Stop Blaming Men For All Of The Problems

How Men's Work Is Changing The World

For The Better

Coach Michael Taylor

Published by Creation Publishing Group LLC

www.creationpublishing.com

© 2024 Michael Taylor

ISBN # 978-8-9857286-4-4

Library of Congress Number # 2024906438

Published and printed in the United States of America.

Table of Contents

Acknowledgements

First, foremost and always, I must acknowledge the source of my creativity and inspiration for writing this book. I choose to call this source, Divine Intelligence. Some may refer to it as, The Creator, God, The Universe, Allah, or a host of other names, however, the name isn't important, what's important is that I recognize it as the source of all creation. As a former Atheist who didn't believe in such a thing, I now know with absolute certainty that Divine Intelligence is real and every human being has access to it. It's been said that skeptics make the best believers and that definitely applies to me. The strong convictions I had that God didn't exists, pales in comparison to the strong conviction and "knowing' that I have knowing God does exist. So, to Divine Intelligence, I simply want to say thank you! Thank you for waking me up to who I was born to be, and for giving me my unique gifts and talents which I now use to help make the world a better place. Sharing my gifts is my way of saying thank you and you know where my heart lies because the love I have for humanity is the love you have for the world.

Back in 2002, I saw a documentary about a program called, The New Warrior Training Adventure hosted by an organization called The Mankind Project. (www.mkp.org) After watching the documentary I decided I wanted to enroll because I resonated with the stories some of the men shared in the documentary about bouncing back from divorce and redefining what it meant to be a man. I signed up for the 3-day workshop and began my journey into discovering what it truly means to be a man. What I learned in the training was I had done everything society says a man was supposed to do to be happy, and yet I was miserable. The training helped me recognize how cultural conditioning had heavily influenced how I viewed being a man, and it provided me with some tools to help me recognize that the key to being happy was to learn how to get in touch with and express my feelings and emotions, and to be willing to heal any unresolved emotional conflicts that kept me from doing so. It was a life changing experience that led me to begin speaking and writing about the changing roles of manhood and masculinity, and this book is the result of more than 25 years of my own growth and transformation.

I am deeply honored that I had the opportunity to meet one of the founders of the New Warrior Training and he has graciously agreed to write the Foreword for this book. His name is Bill Kauth and I'd like to acknowledge him for not only creating the training, but for simply being someone who cares about humanity and decided to do something about making the world a better place. I have the utmost respect and admiration for Bill because he definitely walks his talk when it comes to supporting men in transforming their lives. So, my hats off to you, Bill Kauth, for shining your light into the world and becoming a beacon of hope and transformation for men around the globe.

In men's work, its important that you surround yourself with other men who are committed to redefining manhood and masculinity. Having a support system is an integral part of men's work, so it's important to build a network of men who you can count on and trust as you navigate through the world as a man. I am truly blessed to have several men with whom I can count on and go to for support and I'd like to acknowledge a few of them here.

I'd like to acknowledge Wayne Dawson, Dwayne Klassen, and Boysen Hodgson, for supporting this book by contributing their story about their own transformation. These men are true warriors of male transformation and they are men that I truly love and admire. Thank you men for how you show up in the world and for how you have modeled authentic masculinity for me.

I'd also like to acknowledge and thank Paul Newell and Jermaine Johnson for partnering with me to launch The Brothahood of Kings. We launched the movement in an attempt to get more men of color involved in men's work, and the movement continues to gain momentum and is empowering men of color around the globe. These men are definitely my brothers from other mothers! Love you guys!

And to all the courageous men who would read a book like this, let me acknowledge you for your commitment to your own growth and transformation. Know that you are not alone and there are countless men out there who can and will support you in your growth. So stay focused and committed to your growth and transformation and recognize that your life can become extraordinary if you're willing to put in the work to change your life.

You got this!

Foreword

By: Bill Kauth

Allow me to introduce a delightfully atypical book. Michael Taylor's creation seems to be all about men and a celebration of men, yet it's so much more. It's like a men's mini encyclopedia, inclusive and comprehensive. It moves from the most prescriptive suggestions like joining a men's group to poetic, spiritual abstractions like the alchemy of divine connection or the cosmic dance of creation.

This book has an oddly repetitious writing style that is often more poetry than prose, offering lyrical invitations to step joyously into very specific new possibilities. Some of the best self-help books I've ever read have been consciously repetitious allowing the readers to recognize wisdom and specific teachings until it becomes part of them. Like massaging it into your brain.

Michael's book goes well beyond changing men - it's fully about changing the world. Most all the themes showing up consistently focus on what men need to learn to heal personally and how that touches the world in a good way. Let me highlight a few of my favorites.

Vulnerability and Authenticity: It's all about the personal inner-work needed for men to become real, present human beings. When we allow ourselves to be vulnerable, we open ourselves up to the possibility of true intimacy. This allows us to cultivate deeper, more meaningful connections with others. Indeed, it's in the embrace of vulnerability and the honoring of authenticity that we find the true essence of our humanity.

Men's Groups: The importance of gathering with a circle of men has been close to my heart for several decades, as this is where we learn to be vulnerable and authentic. As Michael says, building networks of support and empathy will encourage emotional vulnerability. These supportive mini-communities allow men to not be alone as they work together to grow and heal. Strong male allies actively challenge harmful stereotypes and promote healthy masculinity. Little by little, week after week men open consciously into more healthy emotional, sexual and even financial lives. Surrounded by like-minded men who uplift and inspire, provides a sense of connection, belonging, and encouragement along a path towards purpose.

Awakening or self-realization: The journey of spiritual discovery involves many inner visionary qualities. Michael invites us as men to find our true purpose and inner calling. As we cultivate this mindset of purpose, it ignites our passion like a flame that burns eternal, lighting the path to our dreams and illuminating the darkest corners of our souls. And as we live into our purpose and passion we find our service. The spirit of service means recognizing the inherent value in giving back to others, which becomes our sacred communion with the divine.

Changing the World: Michael suggests that as we men challenge the status quo and redefine masculinity, we not only benefit ourselves but also contribute to a more equitable and harmonious world for all. Thus by embracing and living into this new vision of masculinity, we, men can play a vital role in creating a brighter and more compassionate future for ourselves and future generations."

Finally let me mention that Michael, knows full well from his own healing process (which he shares with us right up front) that: "The journey towards vulnerability and authenticity is not for the faint of heart." He's inviting us into a courageous men's journey deep inside our own hearts. Or as he says in his own poetic and up lifting way: "It is within the fertile soil of our inner landscape that seeds of inspiration blossom into captivating narratives and dazzling artistic expressions that resonate with the collective heartbeat of humanity!"

Introduction

Back in 1989, I experienced divorce, bankruptcy, foreclosure, depression and being homeless for two years living out of my car. At one point I even contemplated taking my own life because the pain was so great after losing everything. Fortunately, I was able to rebuild my life, and in all honesty, as I write this today, I am happier now than I've ever been in my life.

At 63, I'm in excellent health, I've been blissfully married for 22 years, I have three grown children who I'm absolutely proud of, I'm a passionate and energetic motivational speaker, I'm the author of 14 books, I host several podcasts, and I'm a certified life coach. By my own definition, my life has become extraordinary.

I share these things not to brag, but to make the point that no matter what you may be going through right now, it is definitely possible for you to turn your life around and to make it extraordinary. I'm living proof of this.

In order to do so, it's important for you to understand, if you want your life to change, you must be willing to change. Change is an inside job so you must understand you must go within or else you will go without. Which means you will go without knowing who you truly are and what you're capable of. You will go without experiencing how amazing life can be and you will go without having inner peace, dynamic health, great relationships, and financial abundance, which are the four pillars of an extraordinary life.

It is my belief that the greatest challenge we have on the planet right now is to redefine manhood and masculinity. I believe the majority of social ills can be eradicated by creating a new paradigm of masculinity. This cannot be accomplished by legislation or regulation; it can only be accomplished by empowering one man at a time to embrace some new and better ways of being and relating as men. In other words, it can only be done one man at a time.

Therefore, this is the intention of this book. To transform the world one man at a time by sharing insights and wisdom that supports men in becoming the best men they can possibly be by creating a new paradigm of masculinity.

Welcome to men's work!

Men are recognizing that they have been forced to conform to a very narrow and rather two-dimensional picture of maleness and manhood that they have never had the freedom to question.
— Andrew Cohen

CHAPTER 1

The Old Paradigm of Masculinity

In a world where traditional notions of masculinity have long held sway, it is time for a shift in perspective. It is crucial for men to embrace a new vision of masculinity that goes beyond outdated stereotypes and harmful expectations. This new vision encourages men to express their emotions openly, seek help when needed, and challenge the rigid gender roles that have constrained them for so long.

By embracing a new vision of masculinity, men can redefine what it means to be strong and resilient. It involves being in touch with one's emotions, practicing empathy and compassion, and valuing vulnerability as a source of strength rather than weakness. This shift opens up possibilities for deeper connections with others, improved mental health, and a more fulfilling sense of self.

Men have long been taught to suppress their emotions, to act tough and invulnerable in the face of adversity. This outdated paradigm of masculinity has led to a myriad of issues, from high rates of depression and suicide among men to a lack of emotional intimacy in relationships. By acknowledging and working through their emotions, men can foster healthier and more authentic connections with themselves and those around them.

Furthermore, redefining masculinity is not just about individual growth but also about dismantling the harmful systems that perpetuate toxic masculinity behaviors. It is about challenging the societal norms that dictate how men should behave, look, and feel, and pushing back against a culture that values stoicism over emotional intelligence.

In this new vision of masculinity, men are encouraged to embrace their full selves, to nurture all aspects of their being – physical, emotional, mental, and spiritual. It is about cultivating a sense of wholeness and balance, where vulnerability is seen as a strength, empathy is prized, and self-care is prioritized.

Ultimately, embracing a new vision of masculinity is a journey of self-discovery, growth, and transformation. It is a path towards becoming more authentic, compassionate, and empowered individuals who can lead by example and inspire positive change in the world around them. It is a call to action for men to redefine what it means to be a man in today's world and to create a future where gender equality and emotional well-being are the norm.

Men who embrace this new vision of masculinity not only empower themselves but also challenge oppressive systems that perpetuate harmful gender stereotypes. By standing in solidarity with women and marginalized communities, these men become allies in the fight for equality and justice. Through their actions and advocacy, they help create a more inclusive and compassionate society where everyone can thrive and flourish.

The journey towards redefining masculinity requires introspection, self-awareness, and a willingness to unlearn harmful behaviors ingrained by society. Men must confront their privilege and actively work to dismantle systems of oppression that benefit them at the expense of others. It is a process of continual growth and accountability, where men must hold themselves and each other to a higher standard of respect, integrity, and empathy.

In challenging the status quo and redefining masculinity, men not only benefit themselves but also contribute to a more equitable and harmonious world for all. It is a courageous and transformative path that requires vulnerability, courage, and a commitment to personal and social change. By embracing this new vision of masculinity, men can play a vital role in creating a brighter and more compassionate future for themselves and future generations to come.

Unpacking the Historical Foundations of Male Dominance

As societies continued to develop and expand, the notion of male dominance became further ingrained in various aspects of life. The rise of organized religion played a significant role in solidifying patriarchal structures, with many religious texts and teachings reinforcing the idea of male superiority and authority over women. This theological justification for male dominance not only permeated religious institutions but also influenced societal norms and values.

Throughout history, the legal system has also been a key mechanism in upholding male dominance. Laws and regulations were often designed to favor men, granting them exclusive rights and privileges in areas such as property ownership, inheritance, and decision-making within the family unit. These legal disparities further entrenched the power dynamics between men and women, perpetuating a cycle of inequality that continues to impact our society today.

In the realm of education, opportunities for intellectual and academic growth were historically limited for women compared to men. Access to education was often restricted for females, with many educational institutions and disciplines being dominated by men. This lack of educational equity not only hindered women's personal and professional development but also perpetuated the belief that men were naturally more capable and deserving of success.

As industrialization and urbanization transformed social structures, the division of labor along gender lines became more pronounced. Men were typically employed in higher-paying and more prestigious roles, while women were relegated to lower-paying and less esteemed positions. This economic disparity reinforced the perception of men as providers and breadwinners, further enhancing the power dynamics that favored male dominance.

In the realm of politics and governance, men have historically held the majority of positions of power and influence. The underrepresentation of women in leadership roles has limited the perspectives and experiences brought to the decision-making process, often resulting in policies and practices that do not fully address the needs and concerns of all members of society. This continued exclusion of women from positions of authority serves to perpetuate the cycle of male dominance in the political sphere.

The roots of male dominance run deep in human history, with patriarchal norms and structures shaping the fabric of society for centuries. From the religious justifications to the legal enforcements and societal expectations, the dominance of men has been pervasive and enduring. Despite progress in challenging traditional gender roles and advocating for gender equality, the legacy of male dominance continues to impact our collective consciousness and shape our interactions.

Moving forward, it is essential to confront and dismantle the entrenched systems that perpetuate male dominance and gender inequality. By promoting inclusivity, diversity, and equity in all aspects of life, we can strive towards a more just and balanced society where all individuals, regardless of gender, have the opportunity to thrive and contribute meaningfully. Only through collective efforts and a collective commitment to challenging the status quo can we create a future where gender no longer dictates power and privilege.

The Impact of Patriarchy on Men and Women

Patriarchy, with its pervasive influence rooted in centuries of societal norms and power dynamics, continues to shape and define the experiences of individuals across gender lines. The entrenched nature of patriarchal systems has resulted in profound consequences for both men and women, perpetuating deep-seated inequalities and reinforcing harmful stereotypes and expectations.

For men, navigating the confines of patriarchy often means upholding notions of traditional masculinity that prioritize strength, stoicism, and dominance. From a young age, boys are socialized to suppress vulnerability and emotions in order to align with societal expectations of what it means to be a man. This pressure to conform to rigid gender roles can lead to internalized struggles with self-expression and identity, as men grapple with the tension between societal norms and their own authentic selves.

Furthermore, the emphasis on competitiveness and power within patriarchal structures can create an environment of toxic masculinity behaviors, where aggression and emotional suppression become normalized behaviors. These toxic masculinity behaviors not only harms men themselves but also perpetuates cycles of violence and domination that can have devastating consequences for individuals and communities.

On the other hand, women experience the impact of patriarchy in a multitude of ways that shape their opportunities, resources, and autonomy. The patriarchal system works to maintain control over women's bodies and choices, relegating them to subordinate positions in various spheres of life. From the wage gap and limited access to leadership positions to the prevalence of gender-based violence and systemic discrimination, women continue to face barriers that hinder their full participation and agency in society.

Moreover, the intersectionality of patriarchy with other forms of oppression, such as racism, classism, and ableism, further compounds the challenges that marginalized individuals face. Women of color, LGBTQ+ individuals, and those with disabilities often experience heightened levels of discrimination and violence within patriarchal structures, highlighting the need for an intersectional approach to addressing systemic inequalities.

In order to dismantle the pervasive influence of patriarchy and create a more equitable and inclusive society, it is essential to challenge the underlying beliefs and systems that uphold gender-based oppression. This requires a collective effort to deconstruct harmful gender norms, promote empathy and understanding, and advocate for policies and practices that support gender equality and justice. By engaging in critical self-reflection and actively working towards dismantling patriarchal systems, we can begin to create a more compassionate and just world where all individuals are valued, respected, and empowered to thrive.

Rethinking Violence and Aggression

In this section, we delve into the toxic manifestations of traditional masculinity that glorify violence and aggression. We explore how these harmful traits have been ingrained in societal expectations of manhood, leading to detrimental consequences for both men and those around them. By challenging the notion that aggression equates to strength and power, we aim to shift the narrative towards a more compassionate and peaceful approach to conflict resolution. Through introspection and dialogue, we encourage readers to confront the root causes of their aggressive tendencies and explore healthier ways of expressing their emotions and asserting their needs.

The glorification of violence and aggression in traditional masculinity originates from deeply rooted societal norms and expectations that have historically valued dominance, control, and suppression of emotions in men. From a young age, boys are often socialized to exhibit stoicism, aggression, and emotional detachment as traits of masculinity, leading to a sense of entitlement to power and control over others. This internalized belief system not only harms men themselves by restricting their emotional expression and vulnerability but also perpetuates cycles of violence in communities and relationships.

Moreover, the expectation for men to be physically strong and tough can create a pressure to prove their masculinity through aggressive behavior, whether in sports, relationships, or conflicts. This pressure to conform to rigid gender stereotypes can result in a lack of empathy and emotional intelligence, making it challenging for men to connect with others on a deeper level and engage in healthy communication. As a result, issues such as toxic masculinity behaviors, gender-based violence, and mental health struggles often go unaddressed and perpetuate harmful cycles of behavior.

To combat these damaging effects of traditional masculinity, it is essential for individuals to engage in critical reflection on their beliefs and behaviors. By examining the ways in which societal norms have influenced their understanding of masculinity, men can begin to dismantle toxic traits and embrace healthier forms of self-expression. This process involves cultivating emotional intelligence, empathy, and a willingness to seek help and support when needed.

Ultimately, by challenging the glorification of violence and aggression in traditional masculinity, individuals can work towards creating a more inclusive and compassionate society that values the full range of human emotions and experiences. By shifting the narrative around manhood to one that celebrates vulnerability, empathy, and peaceful conflict resolution, we can strive towards a more equitable and harmonious world for all genders.

Breaking Free from Emotional Restraints

In a society that often dictates strict expectations for how men should behave, many individuals find themselves grappling with emotional restraints that can hinder their personal growth and well-being. Breaking free from these societal norms and embracing one's emotions is a crucial step towards self-discovery and emotional fulfillment.

Men are often taught from a young age to suppress their emotions, to be strong and stoic in the face of adversity. This can create a toxic cycle where emotions are viewed as a sign of weakness, leading to a lack of emotional expression and an inability to effectively communicate their feelings.

However, it is important for men to recognize that experiencing and expressing emotions is not a sign of weakness, but rather a sign of strength and self-awareness. By allowing themselves to feel their emotions fully, men can develop a deeper understanding of themselves and their relationships with others.

One practical way to break free from emotional restraints is to cultivate emotional intelligence. This involves recognizing and labeling one's emotions, understanding their underlying causes, and developing healthy ways to cope with and express them. This process can empower men to navigate their emotions with confidence and authenticity.

Additionally, seeking support from trusted friends, family members, or mental health professionals can provide a safe space for men to explore their emotions and work through any emotional barriers they may be facing. Building a support network of individuals who encourage emotional vulnerability and open communication can help men break free from emotional restraints and cultivate meaningful and fulfilling relationships.

Moreover, societal constructs that perpetuate toxic masculinity behaviors can further inhibit men from fully connecting with their emotions. These constructs often promote the idea that vulnerability is a sign of weakness, leading men to bury their emotions as a means of conforming to societal expectations. Challenging these harmful beliefs and actively working to dismantle them is essential in creating a more inclusive and emotionally open society for men to thrive in.

The impact of unresolved emotional restraints can manifest in various aspects of men's lives, including their mental and physical health. Research has shown that unaddressed emotional issues can contribute to stress, anxiety, and even physical ailments. By addressing and acknowledging their emotions, men can take proactive steps towards improving their overall well-being and quality of life.

Embracing vulnerability as a strength rather than a weakness is a powerful step towards breaking free from emotional restraints and living a more fulfilling and emotionally rich life. Men who embrace their emotions not only cultivate deeper connections with themselves and others but also pave the way for a more empathetic and compassionate society that values emotional authenticity and vulnerability. By taking the courageous step to break free from emotional restraints, men can truly unlock their fullest potential and lead more fulfilling and authentic lives.

Navigating Relationships in the New Paradigm

Navigating Relationships in the New Paradigm:

In the quest to redefine masculinity, one crucial aspect that requires attention is how men navigate relationships in the modern world.

Traditionally, men have been socialized to prioritize power dynamics and control in their relationships, often reinforcing gender stereotypes and unhealthy patterns of behavior. However, in the new paradigm of masculinity, there is a shift towards fostering equality, mutual respect, and emotional connection in relationships.

Men are encouraged to explore and understand their own emotions and vulnerabilities, which in turn allows them to engage more authentically with their partners. Communication becomes a cornerstone of healthy relationships, with an emphasis on active listening, empathy, and open dialogue. This shift towards emotional intelligence and vulnerability can create a deeper sense of intimacy and connection in relationships, benefiting both partners.

In the new paradigm, there is also a recognition of the importance of dismantling toxic masculinity in relationships. This means challenging rigid gender roles and expectations, promoting consent and boundaries, and fostering a culture of respect and equality. Men are encouraged to support their partners in their personal growth and development, rather than seeking to control or dominate them.

Navigating relationships in the new paradigm of masculinity involves a willingness to unlearn harmful relationship behaviors and attitudes, and instead embrace a mindset of collaboration, partnership, and mutual support. By fostering healthy, respectful, and equal relationships, men can not only improve their own well-being but also contribute to creating a more equitable and compassionate society.

It is essential for men to recognize that vulnerability and emotional openness are not signs of weakness, but rather strengths that can foster deeper connections and more fulfilling relationships. By embracing a more inclusive and empathetic approach to relationships, men can break free from the constraints of traditional gender norms and create spaces where both partners feel valued, heard, and respected.

Furthermore, in the new paradigm of masculinity, there is a growing appreciation for the importance of intersectionality and understanding how various aspects of identity, such as race, sexuality, and socioeconomic status, intersect with gender dynamics in relationships. Men are encouraged to reflect on their privilege and how it impacts their interactions with their partners, as well as to actively work towards dismantling systems of oppression that contribute to inequality and discrimination in relationships.

In this new landscape of masculinity, men are learning to navigate relationships with a greater awareness of how societal influences and power dynamics shape their interactions. By recognizing and challenging harmful patterns of behavior and embracing vulnerability and emotional authenticity, men can cultivate more meaningful and respectful connections with their partners. This shift towards healthier relationships not only benefits individuals but also contributes to a more inclusive and equitable society where all genders can thrive and coexist harmoniously.

Overcoming the Stigma of Mental Health

In this section, we delve into the pervasive stigma surrounding mental health issues and the impact it has on men. The societal expectations that discourage men from seeking help and expressing their emotions openly are deeply entrenched in traditional notions of masculinity. From a young age, boys are often taught to suppress their emotions, to "toughen up," and to avoid showing vulnerability. This conditioning creates a harmful cycle where men feel pressured to deal with their struggles in silence, leading to a reluctance to seek professional help when needed.

The consequences of this stigma are far-reaching. Men may suffer in silence, experiencing feelings of isolation, shame, and inadequacy. They may turn to unhealthy coping mechanisms such as substance abuse or risky behaviors to numb their pain. The reluctance to seek help can also exacerbate mental health conditions, leading to long-term consequences for their overall well-being.

It is crucial to challenge these harmful stereotypes and create a culture of acceptance and support for mental health struggles among men. By encouraging open conversations about emotions and mental well-being, we can help break down the barriers that prevent men from seeking help. Providing education on mental health, normalizing discussions around emotions, and promoting empathy and understanding can all play a role in destigmatizing mental health issues for men.

Men need to know that it is okay to ask for help, to seek therapy, and to prioritize their mental well-being. By breaking free from the constraints of societal expectations, men can empower themselves to take control of their mental health and lead fulfilling, authentic lives. It is time to redefine masculinity to include emotional vulnerability, self-care, and seeking support when needed.

Moreover, it is essential to acknowledge the intersectionality of mental health issues with other aspects of identity, such as race, sexual orientation, and socioeconomic status. Men from marginalized communities may face additional barriers to accessing mental health resources due to systemic inequalities and discrimination. It is critical to address these disparities and ensure that mental health support is inclusive and accessible to all individuals.

Additionally, the role of traditional masculinity in perpetuating harmful behaviors and attitudes towards mental health cannot be overlooked. The pressure on men to conform to narrow definitions of strength and resilience can create barriers to seeking help and expressing vulnerability. By deconstructing these toxic norms and promoting a more holistic view of masculinity that embraces emotional honesty and self-care, we can foster healthier attitudes towards mental health for men.

In conclusion, challenging the stigma surrounding mental health and masculinity is a multi-faceted endeavor that requires societal, cultural, and individual changes. By promoting open dialogue, providing support services, and advocating for systemic change, we can create a more compassionate and inclusive society where all individuals, regardless of gender, feel empowered to prioritize their mental well-being.

The Power of Vulnerability and Authenticity

In a society that often values strength and stoicism in men, the concept of vulnerability and authenticity can seem counterintuitive. However, embracing vulnerability and authenticity can be a powerful tool in creating deep connections with others and fostering personal growth.

When we allow ourselves to be vulnerable, we open ourselves up to the possibility of true intimacy and connection. It requires courage to show our true selves, with all our imperfections and fears, to others. By sharing our vulnerabilities, we invite others to do the same, creating a space for empathy and compassion to thrive.

Vulnerability is often seen as a weakness, but in reality, it is a strength. It takes immense courage to be open and honest about our struggles, fears, and insecurities. When we are vulnerable, we show our humanity and allow others to see us for who we truly are. This raw authenticity creates a deep sense of connection and understanding that is essential for meaningful relationships.

Authenticity, on the other hand, involves staying true to ourselves and our values, even when it may be easier to conform to societal expectations. It's about being genuine and honest in our interactions, without putting on a façade or pretending to be someone we're not. When we are authentic, we invite others to do the same, fostering trust and respect in our relationships.

By embracing vulnerability and authenticity, we can cultivate deeper, more meaningful connections with others. It allows us to break down the barriers and facades that separate us, paving the way for genuine, honest interactions. This vulnerability can lead to profound revelations and emotional healing as we connect with others on a deeper level.

Authenticity, in its purity, allows us to honor our true selves and values. When we embrace our authenticity, we are able to live in alignment with our core beliefs and desires. This genuine expression of self not only fosters stronger relationships but also nurtures our own sense of self-worth and inner peace.

Together, vulnerability and authenticity create a rich tapestry of connection and understanding in our lives. By being brave enough to show our true selves and stand firmly in our values, we can create a world where we are truly seen and accepted for who we are. This journey of vulnerability and authenticity is a profound one, leading us to a place of deep connection, personal growth, and genuine fulfillment.

Rewriting the Narrative of Success

In a world where traditional notions of success often equate to material wealth, status, and power, it is crucial to redefine what success truly means. The current narrative of success is deeply ingrained in our society, perpetuated by media, culture, and societal expectations. This narrow definition often leads to immense pressure to achieve external markers of success, leaving many feeling unfulfilled and inadequate.

Rewriting the narrative of success involves shifting our focus from external validation to internal fulfillment. It requires us to redefine success on our own terms, based on our values, passions, and goals. True success is not about comparing ourselves to others or meeting societal standards, but about living authentically and in alignment with our true selves.

By reevaluating our priorities and shifting our mindset, we can create a new paradigm of success that prioritizes holistic well-being, personal growth, and meaningful relationships. Success should be measured by our ability to live with purpose, integrity, and joy, rather than by external markers of achievement.

Embracing this new narrative of success allows us to break free from the constraints of societal expectations and pursue a path that is true to who we are. It empowers us to define success on our own terms and to create a life that is fulfilling, meaningful, and in alignment with our deepest values.

When we redefine success in this way, we open ourselves up to a world of possibilities and opportunities. We begin to see success as a journey rather than a destination, as a continuous process of growth and self-discovery. This new perspective encourages us to embrace challenges, learn from failures, and celebrate our achievements, no matter how small.

Living a successful life, by our own definition, requires courage, resilience, and a willingness to step outside our comfort zone. It means being true to ourselves, even when faced with criticism or doubt. It means cultivating a sense of gratitude for the present moment and maintaining a positive attitude in the face of adversity.

Ultimately, true success is not about reaching a specific goal or attaining a certain level of status. It is about living with meaning, purpose, and authenticity. It is about cultivating inner peace, self-acceptance, and a deep sense of fulfillment that transcends external circumstances.

As we continue to rewrite the narrative of success, let us remember that our worth is not determined by external measures, but by the depth of our character, the kindness in our hearts, and the authenticity of our actions. Let us strive to redefine success in a way that aligns with our values and brings us closer to our true selves.

In this journey of self-discovery and redefining success, we must also acknowledge the importance of embracing failure. Failure is not a sign of weakness or inadequacy but a stepping stone towards growth and learning. It is through failure that we gain resilience, perseverance, and humility. By shifting our perspective on failure, we can see it as an opportunity for growth and transformation, rather than a barrier to success.

Furthermore, it is essential to cultivate a sense of gratitude in our lives. Gratitude enables us to appreciate the present moment, acknowledge our blessings, and find joy in the simple things. It allows us to shift our focus from what we lack to what we have, fostering a sense of abundance and contentment.

As we navigate the complexities of defining our own version of success, we must also prioritize self-care and well-being. Taking care of our physical, mental, and emotional health is essential for long-term success and fulfillment. Prioritizing self-care practices such as mindfulness, exercise, and healthy relationships nurtures our overall well-being and resilience.

In essence, the journey of redefining success is a deeply personal and transformative process. It requires introspection, courage, and a willingness to challenge societal norms. By embracing our true selves, living with purpose and authenticity, and cultivating a mindset of growth and gratitude, we can redefine success in a way that is meaningful, fulfilling, and aligned with our deepest values.

Cultivating a Culture of Support and Empowerment

In this section, we delve into the importance of creating a culture that values support and empowerment for all individuals, regardless of gender. Traditional notions of masculinity have often placed undue pressure on men to embody traits such as strength, stoicism, and independence, leading to a lack of emphasis on seeking help or expressing vulnerability. This societal expectation can have detrimental effects on men's mental health, as they may feel isolated or unable to share their struggles with others.

Shifting towards a more inclusive and supportive environment can benefit individuals of all genders. By fostering a culture that encourages open communication and seeks to break down the stigma surrounding mental health, we can create a space where men feel comfortable seeking assistance when needed. This can lead to improved emotional well-being and resilience, as individuals are able to access the support they require to navigate life's challenges.

Community and connection play a vital role in promoting mental well-being. By building networks of support and empathy, individuals can feel a sense of belonging and understanding that is crucial for maintaining good mental health. Encouraging men to engage in meaningful relationships and to seek help from trusted sources can help combat feelings of isolation and foster a sense of community that is essential for overall well-being.

Furthermore, the power of mentorship and role modeling cannot be understated in shaping positive norms and behaviors. Strong male allies who actively challenge harmful stereotypes and promote healthy masculinity can make a significant impact in creating a more equitable and supportive society. By demonstrating empathy, compassion, and a willingness to seek help when needed, these allies can set an example for others to follow and help create a culture that values emotional growth and self-care.

In the modern era, discussions around gender and masculinity have evolved to encompass a more nuanced understanding of the complex interplay between societal expectations and individual well-being. Men today are increasingly recognizing the importance of prioritizing their mental health and seeking help when facing challenges. Movements advocating for mental health awareness and breaking down toxic stereotypes have gained momentum, creating space for men to express vulnerability and seek support without fear of judgment or stigma.

Moreover, research has highlighted the intersectionality of masculinity with other aspects of identity, such as race, sexual orientation, and socio-economic status. Men from marginalized communities may face unique challenges in navigating expectations around masculinity, further underscoring the need for inclusive and intersectional approaches to supporting men's mental health. By acknowledging and addressing these intersecting factors, we can better understand the diverse experiences of men and work towards creating more equitable and supportive environments for all individuals.

In conclusion, by working together to challenge outdated notions of masculinity and promote a culture of respect and support, we can create a more inclusive and compassionate world for everyone. Embracing vulnerability, seeking help when needed, and fostering connections with others are essential steps towards promoting mental well-being and building a society that values the well-being of all individuals, regardless of gender.

*To me the definition of true masculinity -
and femininity, too - is being able to lay in
your own skin comfortably.*
— Vincent D'Onofrio

CHAPTER 2

A New Paradigm of Masculinity

Embracing Change: The Evolution of Masculinity

In our rapidly changing world, the concept of masculinity is undergoing a profound evolution. Traditional notions of what it means to be a man are being challenged and redefined, leading to a shift in how men view themselves and their roles in society.

Men are increasingly recognizing the importance of emotional intelligence and vulnerability, understanding that true strength lies in the ability to express their feelings and seek help when needed. This shift away from the stoic, unemotional stereotype of masculinity is opening up new opportunities for men to connect with others on a deeper level and forge more meaningful relationships.

The changing landscape of masculinity also involves a reevaluation of power dynamics and traditional gender roles. Men are questioning outdated notions of dominance and control, and instead are embracing collaboration and equality in their interactions with others. This shift towards a more balanced and inclusive approach to masculinity is not only benefiting men themselves but also contributing to a more harmonious and equitable society as a whole.

Men today are facing a paradoxical challenge – on one hand, they are encouraged to be emotionally available and vulnerable, while on the other hand, they are still bombarded with societal expectations of traditional masculinity that promote toughness, aggression, and dominance. This duality can create internal conflicts for men as they navigate between expressing their authentic emotions and conforming to societal norms.

Moreover, the intersectionality of masculinity with other aspects of identity, such as race, sexuality, and socioeconomic status, adds further complexity to the evolving concept of what it means to be a man. Men from marginalized communities often face unique challenges and pressures that shape their experiences of masculinity in distinct ways, highlighting the need for a more inclusive and intersectional approach to redefining masculinity.

As men continue to grapple with these multifaceted dynamics of masculinity, it becomes increasingly important for individuals and society as a whole to engage in open dialogue, reflection, and education to break free from limiting stereotypes and create a more compassionate and inclusive understanding of what it means to be a man in the 21st century. Only through collective effort and a commitment to authenticity and empathy can men truly embrace a healthier and more empowering vision of masculinity that benefits themselves and the world around them.

The Impact of the Feminist Movement on Men

One key aspect of the feminist movement's impact on men is the questioning of traditional notions of strength and vulnerability. Historically, men have been expected to be strong, stoic, and in control at all times. However, the feminist movement has highlighted the importance of emotional expression and the acceptance of vulnerability as essential components of masculinity. Men are now being encouraged to explore their emotions, seek support when needed, and reject the idea that showing vulnerability is a sign of weakness.

Moreover, the feminist movement has drawn attention to the harmful effects of toxic masculinity - a set of behaviors and attitudes that promote aggression, dominance, and the objectification of women. Men who align themselves with feminist principles are urged to challenge these toxic behaviors within themselves and in society at large. By dismantling toxic masculinity, men can create healthier, more respectful relationships with others and foster a more inclusive and equitable society.

Furthermore, the feminist movement has underscored the importance of intersectionality in understanding the complex ways in which gender intersects with other identities such as race, class, sexuality, and ability. Men need to recognize that their experiences of privilege and power are shaped by these intersecting identities and work towards dismantling systems of oppression that harm not only women but also marginalized groups within the male community.

In essence, the impact of the feminist movement on men is a call to introspection, growth, and action. By embracing feminist principles and challenging traditional notions of masculinity, men have the opportunity to create a more inclusive, equitable, and compassionate world for all individuals, irrespective of gender.

Additionally, the feminist movement has also highlighted the importance of men's role as allies in the fight for gender equality. Men are encouraged to listen to and amplify the voices of women, support women's leadership, and actively work towards dismantling patriarchal systems that perpetuate gender inequality. By being active allies, men can contribute to creating a more just and equitable society for all individuals.

Furthermore, the feminist movement has shed light on the issue of societal expectations and pressures that affect men's mental health and well-being. Men are often socialized to suppress their emotions, leading to mental health struggles such as depression and anxiety. By embracing feminist ideals of emotional expression and vulnerability, men can prioritize their mental health and work towards breaking down harmful stereotypes that contribute to mental health stigma.

Moreover, the feminist movement emphasizes the importance of consent and respect in all interactions. Men are called to challenge notions of entitlement and power dynamics in relationships, promoting mutual respect and communication. By fostering healthy and equitable relationships, men can contribute to building a more harmonious and respectful society for all individuals.

In conclusion, the feminist movement's impact on men is multifaceted, calling for a reexamination of traditional masculinity, the dismantling of toxic behaviors, the recognition of intersectional identities, the role of allies in gender equality, prioritizing mental health, and promoting healthy relationships. By embracing feminist principles, men have the opportunity to transform themselves, their communities, and society as a whole towards greater inclusivity, equity, and compassion.

Redefining Success: Breaking Free from Traditional Gender Norms

In the midst of this transformative shift in the definition of success for men lies a profound opportunity for personal growth and introspection. Men are increasingly recognizing the limitations of society's narrow expectations and are embarking on a journey of self-discovery to uncover their true values and priorities.

This journey often involves a reevaluation of long-held beliefs and attitudes towards success. Men are questioning the traditional measures of success that have been ingrained in them from an early age, such as financial wealth or career status. Instead, they are seeking a more holistic approach that encompasses not only professional accomplishments but also personal fulfillment, emotional well-being, and meaningful connections with others.

Central to this new paradigm of success is the recognition of the interconnectedness of different aspects of life. Men are understanding that true fulfillment cannot be achieved by excelling in just one area while neglecting others. Rather, success is a delicate balance that requires nurturing one's mental, emotional, and physical health alongside their professional pursuits.

In this process of redefining success, men are embracing vulnerability and authenticity as powerful tools for growth. By acknowledging their emotions and vulnerabilities, men are fostering deeper connections with themselves and others, leading to more meaningful and fulfilling relationships. This shift towards emotional intelligence and empathy is not only beneficial for individuals but also for the broader community, fostering a culture of compassion and understanding.

Moreover, the evolving concept of masculinity is paving the way for men to express a wider range of emotions and experiences without fear of judgment or stigma. Men are learning to embrace their complexity and individuality, rejecting the rigid stereotypes that have long constrained them. This newfound freedom to express their authentic selves is empowering men to live more authentically and boldly, unapologetically embracing their unique perspectives and values.

As men continue on this transformative journey of self-discovery and redefinition of success, they are shaping a future in which masculinity is more inclusive, empathetic, and compassionate. By challenging societal expectations and embracing their true selves, men are forging a new path towards a more balanced and fulfilling life, one that prioritizes well-being, authenticity, and meaningful connections above all else.

The Rise of the Stay-at-Home Dad

In recent years, there has been a noticeable shift in the traditional roles of parenting, with more and more fathers choosing to stay at home and take on the primary caregiving responsibilities. This trend of stay-at-home dads is challenging the societal norms that dictate mothers should be the primary caregivers while fathers go out to work.

The rise of the stay-at-home dad can be attributed to various factors, including changes in societal expectations, economic conditions, and shifting perspectives on gender roles. In today's fast-paced society, there is a growing emphasis on work-life balance and the importance of being present for one's family. Many fathers are recognizing that they can play a vital role in raising their children and are choosing to prioritize their family over their careers.

One key benefit of having a stay-at-home dad is the opportunity for children to develop a strong bond with their father. Research has shown that involved fathers positively impact children's cognitive development, emotional well-being, and social skills. By being actively engaged in caregiving tasks, stay-at-home dads can provide a nurturing and supportive environment that enhances their children's overall growth and development.

Moreover, the presence of a stay-at-home dad in the family dynamic can challenge traditional gender stereotypes and promote gender equality within the household. Children raised in households where caregiving responsibilities are shared between both parents are more likely to develop a broader understanding of gender roles and dynamics. This can lead to greater empathy, respect, and equality in their future relationships and interactions with others.

Despite the numerous benefits of having a stay-at-home dad, there are challenges that these fathers may face. Society's expectations around gender roles and parenting norms can lead to stigma, judgment, or isolation for stay-at-home dads. They may also struggle with feelings of identity loss or a lack of recognition for their caregiving role. It's essential to recognize and support the valuable contribution that stay-at-home dads make to their families and communities.

In conclusion, the rising trend of stay-at-home dads represents a positive and progressive shift towards a more inclusive and equitable approach to parenting. By breaking down traditional barriers and embracing shared responsibilities within the family, stay-at-home dads are helping to reshape societal perceptions of caregiving and promoting a more balanced and fulfilling family life for all.

Finding Fulfillment in Intimate Relationships

In a society where traditional gender roles and expectations have long dictated how men should behave in relationships, many men are now exploring new ways to find fulfillment and connection in their intimate partnerships. Gone are the days when men were expected to be stoic and emotionally distant; today's men are seeking meaningful and authentic connections with their partners.

Open and honest communication stands as the cornerstone of building and maintaining healthy relationships. Men are learning to navigate their emotions and express their needs with vulnerability and authenticity. By fostering a safe space for open dialogue, men can share their thoughts, fears, and desires with their partners, leading to a deeper understanding and connection between them.

Emotional intimacy, often overlooked in past generations, is now given the attention it deserves. Men are recognizing the profound impact of emotional connection on their relationships. By actively listening, offering empathy, and showing support, men can strengthen the emotional bond with their partners, creating a solid foundation for a fulfilling and lasting partnership.

Moreover, the shift towards equality and partnership in relationships is gaining momentum. Men are acknowledging the importance of collaboration, shared responsibilities, and mutual respect in their intimate connections. By embracing a partnership model, where both individuals contribute equally to the relationship dynamics, men can cultivate a sense of teamwork and unity with their partners.

Beyond traditional gender norms, men are encouraged to explore their own identities and redefine masculinity in the context of modern relationships. By breaking free from stereotypes and embracing vulnerability, men can forge deeper connections with their partners based on authenticity, honesty, and emotional depth.

Navigating the complexities of modern relationships, men are also learning the importance of self-awareness and personal growth. By examining their own patterns, beliefs, and behaviors, men can cultivate a deeper understanding of themselves and their needs within a relationship. This introspective journey allows men to develop a greater sense of empathy, compassion, and emotional intelligence, strengthening their ability to connect with their partners on a profound level.

Furthermore, men are recognizing the significance of active listening and empathy in fostering healthy and fulfilling relationships. By tuning into their partner's needs, emotions, and experiences, men can demonstrate care, understanding, and validation, creating a supportive and nurturing environment for intimacy to flourish.

In the realm of modern relationships, men are also embracing the concept of emotional labor and shared responsibilities. Recognizing that emotional support, household chores, and childcare are not solely the domain of women, men are stepping up to actively participate in all aspects of the relationship. By sharing the emotional and practical burdens of the partnership, men are fostering a sense of equality, reciprocity, and mutual respect with their partners.

Ultimately, finding fulfillment in intimate relationships as a man requires a commitment to growth, self-awareness, empathy, and vulnerability. By embracing these principles and engaging in ongoing personal and relational development, men can cultivate deep, enriching connections with their partners, leading to profound satisfaction, fulfillment, and lasting love in their intimate partnerships.

Active Fatherhood: Nurturing the Next Generation

In today's rapidly evolving world, the role of fathers and the concept of fatherhood have undergone significant transformations. Gone are the days when fathers were predominantly seen as breadwinners and disciplinarians. Modern fathers are actively involved in nurturing and raising their children, playing a crucial role in shaping the next generation.

Active fatherhood is not just about providing for the material needs of their children; it's about being emotionally present, actively engaged, and supportive in the upbringing of their kids. Research has shown that children who have involved fathers tend to have better emotional and social development, perform better in school, and have higher self-esteem.

The evolution of fatherhood is deeply rooted in societal changes, including shifts in gender roles, changing family dynamics, and the recognition of the importance of male involvement in child development. In the past, fathers were often expected to be distant authority figures, while mothers were primarily responsible for nurturing and caregiving. However, as our understanding of parenting roles has evolved, we now acknowledge the unique contributions that fathers can make to their children's lives.

Active fatherhood goes beyond traditional caregiving tasks to encompass emotional support, positive role modeling, and creating a secure and loving environment for children to thrive. Fathers who actively engage with their children provide them with a sense of security, stability, and confidence that helps them navigate the challenges of childhood and adolescence.

Balancing the demands of work and family life can be a daunting task for many fathers. Finding the time and energy to be present and engaged with their children while juggling responsibilities can be a constant struggle. However, investing in quality time with your children, even in small moments, can have a lasting impact on their well-being and development.

Communication is a cornerstone of active fatherhood. By listening attentively to their children, fathers can foster trust, build strong relationships, and create open lines of communication. Encouraging children to express their thoughts, feelings, and ideas without judgment helps them develop strong self-esteem and emotional intelligence.

Each father-child relationship is unique, and active fatherhood may look different for each family. The key is to be present, involved, and supportive, demonstrating love, respect, and guidance to your children. By embracing the evolving role of fatherhood and actively engaging in your child's life, you can make a profound impact on their growth, well-being, and future success.

Furthermore, the concept of active fatherhood extends beyond the immediate family unit. Fathers also play a crucial role in shaping societal attitudes towards gender roles and parenting. By challenging traditional stereotypes and outdated norms, fathers can help create a more inclusive and supportive society for future generations. Through their actions and behaviors, fathers can demonstrate the importance of empathy, respect, and equality in all aspects of life.

In essence, active fatherhood is a multifaceted and evolving concept that requires continuous reflection, growth, and adaptation. By embracing the complexities of modern fatherhood and actively engaging with their children, fathers can leave a lasting legacy of love, compassion, and empowerment for generations to come.

Pursuing Passion and Purpose in Career Choices

In today's rapidly changing world, men are increasingly finding themselves drawn to careers that align with their passion and purpose. The traditional notions of success, such as climbing the corporate ladder or chasing after material wealth, are being redefined as men seek deeper fulfillment and meaning in their professional lives.

This shift towards purpose-driven careers reflects a broader societal trend towards introspection and authenticity. Men are no longer satisfied with simply going through the motions in their jobs; they are searching for work that allows them to make a positive impact on the world and contribute to something greater than themselves.

In this quest for purpose, men are often willing to take risks and step outside of their comfort zones. They understand that true fulfillment often lies beyond the confines of a stable job or a lucrative paycheck. By aligning their career choices with their values and interests, men are able to tap into a deeper sense of motivation and passion that drives them towards success.

Finding a career that aligns with one's passion and purpose is not always easy. It may require courage to leave behind a familiar path or financial security in pursuit of something more meaningful. However, the rewards of such a journey are profound. Men who are able to follow their passion and purpose in their careers often report higher levels of job satisfaction, increased creativity and productivity, and a greater sense of overall well-being.

Moreover, men who prioritize purpose in their careers often experience a higher level of job engagement and longevity. When individuals feel connected to the greater mission of their work, they are more likely to remain dedicated and committed, even in the face of challenges or setbacks. This sense of purpose can provide a powerful source of motivation and resilience, helping men navigate the ups and downs of their professional lives with a sense of clarity and determination.

Ultimately, choosing a purpose-driven career is not just a professional decision but a personal one as well. Men who align their work with their values and passions are able to live more authentically and genuinely, bringing a sense of fulfillment that transcends the confines of the workplace. By embracing their purpose and striving towards meaningful goals, men have the opportunity to not only succeed professionally but to lead a life that is deeply meaningful and rewarding on a holistic level.

Embracing Emotional Wellness: The Power of Therapy

In a society that often emphasizes stoicism and emotional suppression, many men are starting to recognize the value of prioritizing their emotional well-being. Therapy has emerged as a powerful tool for men to explore their feelings, confront underlying issues, and develop healthier coping mechanisms.

Contrary to the stereotype that seeking therapy is a sign of weakness, more and more men are embracing the idea that mental health is just as important as physical health. By engaging in therapy, men can gain a better understanding of themselves, address unresolved trauma or emotional wounds, and learn effective ways to manage stress and anxiety.

Therapy provides a safe and confidential space for men to express their thoughts and emotions without fear of judgment. Through open and honest dialogue with a trained therapist, men can work through challenges, develop self-awareness, and cultivate a greater sense of emotional resilience.

Additionally, therapy can help men improve their relationships with others by enhancing communication skills, fostering empathy, and building stronger connections. By addressing mental health concerns and learning healthy coping strategies, men can improve their overall well-being and lead more fulfilling lives.

Furthermore, the societal pressure on men to adhere to traditional masculine norms can contribute to feelings of isolation and inadequacy. Therapy offers a supportive environment where men can explore these expectations, challenge harmful beliefs, and redefine what it means to be a man in today's world.

Men who have experienced trauma, such as childhood abuse or combat-related PTSD, can benefit immensely from therapy. Trauma-informed therapy approaches, such as cognitive-behavioral therapy (CBT) or Eye Movement Desensitization and Reprocessing (EMDR), can help men process their experiences, manage symptoms, and reclaim a sense of control over their lives.

Moreover, therapy can also assist men in developing healthy coping mechanisms for stress, anxiety, and other mental health challenges. By learning techniques such as mindfulness, relaxation exercises, and cognitive restructuring, men can build resilience and adaptability in the face of life's difficulties.

In essence, embracing emotional wellness through therapy is not a sign of weakness, but a courageous step towards self-improvement and personal growth. By prioritizing their mental health and seeking support when needed, men can break free from the confines of societal expectations and cultivate a greater sense of emotional balance and fulfillment in their lives.

A New Generation of Men: Less Materialism, More Meaning

In a world where materialism and consumerism have long been considered markers of success, a new generation of men is emerging with a different set of values. These men are shifting their focus away from accumulating wealth and possessions, and instead, they are prioritizing experiences, relationships, and personal growth.

Gone are the days when material possessions defined a man's worth. Instead, these men are seeking fulfillment in the intangible aspects of life – deep connections with others, meaningful work, and a sense of purpose. They understand that true happiness cannot be bought with money or status, but rather, it comes from living authentically and aligning their actions with their values.

This shift towards less materialism and more meaning has profound implications for society as a whole. Men who prioritize relationships and personal growth are more likely to be empathetic, compassionate, and socially conscious. They are committed to making a positive impact on the world and are willing to challenge outdated norms and expectations in pursuit of a more just and equitable society.

As this new generation of men continues to redefine masculinity and embrace a values-based approach to life, they are paving the way for a more authentic and fulfilling existence for themselves and future generations. By choosing meaning over materialism, these men are redefining success on their terms and inspiring others to do the same.

This shift is not just a passing trend but a fundamental reevaluation of what it means to live a meaningful life. Men are realizing that true fulfillment lies in the quality of their relationships, the impact they have on others, and their own personal growth journey. They are rejecting the pressure to define themselves by their possessions or status, recognizing that these external markers are fleeting and ultimately unfulfilling.

In embracing a values-based approach, these men are cultivating a sense of authenticity and purpose that transcends societal expectations and traditional notions of success. They are challenging the status quo, redefining masculinity, and creating a new paradigm for future generations to aspire to.

The ripple effects of this shift are far-reaching, extending beyond individual lives to reshape societal norms and values. As men prioritize connection, personal growth, and making a positive impact, they are contributing to a more compassionate, empathetic, and equitable world. This values-based approach to life is not just about personal fulfillment but about creating a more harmonious and sustainable future for all.

Building a Brighter Future: The Path Forward for Men

In a rapidly changing world, the path forward for men involves embracing a new paradigm of masculinity that prioritizes equality, empathy, and personal growth. Men are increasingly recognizing the importance of challenging traditional gender roles and contributing to a more just and equitable society.

As we move towards a brighter future, it is essential for men to engage in self-reflection and introspection. This involves questioning ingrained beliefs and behaviors that may perpetuate harmful stereotypes or limit personal development. By cultivating a sense of awareness and mindfulness, men can begin to break free from societal expectations and forge their own paths.

Part of building a brighter future for men involves supporting and uplifting one another. By forming strong connections with other men and fostering a sense of community, individuals can find encouragement and validation in their journey towards personal growth. This sense of camaraderie can also lead to collective action and advocacy for positive change in society.

Central to the path forward for men is the recognition of the value of emotional intelligence and vulnerability. By embracing their emotions and seeking support when needed, men can cultivate healthier relationships and a deeper sense of self-awareness. This openness to vulnerability not only strengthens personal connections but also contributes to a more authentic and fulfilling life.

Furthermore, men must actively challenge toxic masculinity and work towards creating a culture of respect and inclusivity. This involves speaking out against violence, discrimination, and harmful attitudes that perpetuate gender-based oppression. By becoming allies in the fight for gender equality, men can help create a more compassionate and understanding world for all.

Men's journey towards a more enlightened masculinity also involves unpacking the intersectionality of their identities. Recognizing how factors such as race, sexual orientation, and socioeconomic status intersect with gender can lead to a more nuanced understanding of privilege, power dynamics, and systemic inequalities. By engaging in conversations about privilege and actively working to dismantle oppressive structures, men can contribute to a more equitable and inclusive society for all individuals.

Moreover, men must actively challenge the narrative that equates strength with emotional detachment and vulnerability with weakness. By embracing a more expansive definition of masculinity that values authenticity, empathy, and sensitivity, men can cultivate deeper connections with themselves and others. This shift towards a more emotionally intelligent and compassionate masculinity not only benefits individual well-being but also fosters healthier relationships and a more harmonious society.

In essence, the path forward for men is a multifaceted journey of personal growth, social consciousness, and advocacy for gender equality. By embracing change, challenging norms, and prioritizing empathy and self-awareness, men can play a vital role in creating a more inclusive and equitable world for all.

I do not believe toxic masculinity actually exists. People confuse toxic masculinity with toxic behaviors and they are not the same thing. Toxic masculinity occurs when a man is out of touch with authentic masculinity. A man who is in touch with authentic masculinity will never act out with toxic behaviors.
— Coach Michael Taylor

CHAPTER 3

The Myth of Toxic Masculinity

Rethinking Toxic Masculinity

In today's society, the concept of toxic masculinity has become a topic of heated discussion and debate. Traditionally, masculinity has been associated with strength, independence, and dominance. However, this narrow definition has often led to harmful behaviors and attitudes that can have serious consequences for both men and those around them.

Toxic masculinity operates within a framework of rigid gender norms that dictate how men are expected to behave. From a young age, boys are bombarded with messages that reinforce the idea that to be a "real man," they must be tough, strong, and in control. This pressure to conform to a limited and unrealistic ideal of masculinity can have profound effects on men's mental health and overall well-being.

Men who internalize toxic masculine norms often find themselves trapped in a cycle of emotional suppression and self-denial. The stigma surrounding vulnerability and seeking help for mental health issues can lead to feelings of isolation and shame. As a result, many men struggle silently with their emotions, leading to increased rates of depression, anxiety, and substance abuse. The reluctance to seek support or express their feelings can have devastating consequences, as men may turn to harmful coping mechanisms or become more prone to engaging in risky behaviors.

Moreover, toxic masculinity perpetuates harmful power dynamics and reinforces gender inequality. By elevating qualities like aggression, dominance, and control as markers of manhood, toxic masculinity can fuel a culture of violence and discrimination. Men who conform to these toxic norms may feel compelled to assert their dominance through harmful behaviors, contributing to a cycle of harm that perpetuates harmful stereotypes about masculinity. This not only harms men themselves but also impacts their relationships with others, perpetuating harmful dynamics within families, friendships, and communities.

It is essential to recognize that toxic masculinity is a social construct that can be unlearned and reshaped. Men have the capacity to redefine masculinity and create healthier, more inclusive expressions of manhood. By challenging outdated beliefs and promoting positive models of masculinity that value empathy, emotional intelligence, and respectful communication, we can foster a culture that uplifts and supports all individuals on their journey towards self-discovery and personal growth.

To combat toxic masculinity, individuals must engage in ongoing self-reflection and introspection. This process may involve challenging deeply ingrained beliefs about masculinity, exploring new ways of expressing emotions and building connections, and actively working to dismantle harmful patterns of behavior. By cultivating a more expansive and inclusive understanding of masculinity, we can create a world where all individuals, regardless of gender, can thrive and flourish authentically.

Understanding Authentic Masculinity

In today's society, the concept of masculinity continues to be a topic of great importance and complexity. Men are often bombarded with conflicting messages about what it means to be a man, leading to confusion and inner turmoil. The traditional notions of masculinity that have been perpetuated for generations often center around qualities like stoicism, aggression, and dominance. While these traits can have their place in certain contexts, they should not define the entirety of masculinity.

Authentic masculinity, on the other hand, delves deeper into the multi-dimensional nature of what it truly means to be a man. It goes beyond the superficial expectations and societal norms to explore the essence of one's individuality and essence. Authentic masculinity requires a man to be in tune with his inner self, acknowledging and accepting his emotions and vulnerabilities as integral parts of his identity. It is a process of self-discovery and self-acceptance that allows a man to embrace his complexities and contradictions without fear or shame.

One key aspect of authentic masculinity is the understanding that strength comes in many forms. While physical prowess and assertiveness are often glorified as symbols of masculinity, true strength lies in the ability to be vulnerable and open. A man who is secure in his masculinity is unafraid to show compassion, empathy, and kindness towards others. He understands that these qualities do not diminish his manhood but enhance it, creating deeper connections and fostering a sense of community and understanding.

Moreover, authentic masculinity recognizes the importance of self-reflection and personal growth. A man who is committed to living authentically continually seeks to learn and evolve, challenging his preconceived notions and biases. He understands that true masculinity is not about conforming to external expectations but about embracing his unique journey and celebrating the diversity of masculinity in all its forms.

Furthermore, authentic masculinity involves breaking free from the constraints of toxic masculinity, which can limit men's emotional expression and hinder their ability to form meaningful relationships. By dismantling these harmful stereotypes and embracing a more inclusive and empathetic approach to manhood, individuals can create healthier and more fulfilling connections with themselves and others.

In essence, authentic masculinity is a journey of self-discovery, acceptance, and growth that transcends societal expectations and embraces the complexity of the human experience. It is about redefining what it means to be a man in a world that is constantly evolving and challenging traditional norms. By embracing his true self, honoring his emotions and vulnerabilities, and fostering empathy and compassion, a man can cultivate a deeper understanding of his masculinity and create a more authentic and fulfilling life for himself and those around him.

The Energy of Masculinity and Femininity

In the intricate tapestry of human existence, the dance of masculine and feminine energies weaves a complex web of influences that shape our experiences, relationships, and sense of self. Masculinity and femininity are not mere societal constructs; they are primal forces that reside within each of us, regardless of gender identity. Understanding and embracing the interplay of these energies can lead to profound personal transformation and spiritual growth.

Masculine energy, with its assertiveness and drive, often takes center stage in a world that values action and achievement. It is the fire that propels us forward, urging us to overcome challenges and reach for our dreams. However, when unbalanced, unchecked masculinity can manifest as aggression, dominance, and a disconnect from the softer, more nurturing aspects of our being.

Feminine energy, with its intuitive wisdom and emotional depth, offers a counterpoint to the masculine drive for action. It is the water that flows through our souls, nourishing our creativity, compassion, and capacity for empathy. Yet, in a society that often devalues the feminine, we may struggle to tap into these qualities, fearing they make us look weak or vulnerable.

The key to unlocking our full potential lies in embracing both our masculine and feminine energies in harmony. By integrating the strength and courage of the masculine with the sensitivity and intuition of the feminine, we can cultivate a sense of wholeness that transcends societal norms and expectations. This balance allows us to approach life with clarity, compassion, and authenticity, leading to deeper connections with ourselves and others.

In this sacred union of masculine and feminine energies within us, we discover a reservoir of power and creativity that knows no bounds. It is through honoring and integrating these dual aspects of our nature that we can access a deeper level of self-awareness, emotional intelligence, and spiritual enlightenment. We come to realize that true strength lies not in dominating others, but in embracing our vulnerabilities and connecting with the world from a place of authenticity and love.

As we continue on our journey of self-discovery and personal evolution, let us remember that the harmonious balance of masculine and feminine energies is not a destination but a lifelong process of growth and transformation. By nurturing both aspects of ourselves and seeking alignment with our inner truth, we can embody the full spectrum of human potential and radiate our light out into the world, inspiring others to do the same.

Exploring Toxic Behaviors

In addition to the visible manifestations of toxic masculinity, there are also subtler ways in which these harmful behaviors can manifest. One key aspect to consider is the link between toxic masculinity and the perpetuation of gender-based violence. Research has shown that men who adhere strongly to traditional masculine ideals are more likely to engage in behaviors that are harmful to themselves and others, including aggression and violence. This can have serious consequences for individuals and communities, leading to increased rates of domestic violence, sexual assault, and other forms of gender-based violence.

Furthermore, toxic masculinity can also contribute to mental health issues among men. The pressure to conform to rigid gender norms can create significant emotional distress and internal conflict for individuals who do not fit the traditional mold of masculinity. Men may feel pressure to suppress their emotions, leading to feelings of isolation and inadequacy. This, in turn, can contribute to higher rates of depression, anxiety, and other mental health disorders among men.

Another important aspect to consider is the impact of toxic masculinity on relationships. When men are socialized to prioritize dominance and control, it can hinder the development of healthy and equitable partnerships. Men who exhibit toxic behaviors may struggle to communicate effectively, show empathy, or establish trust in their relationships. This can lead to power imbalances, conflict, and ultimately, the breakdown of relationships.

To combat toxic masculinity, it is essential to engage in critical dialogue about gender norms and expectations. This includes educating individuals about the harmful effects of rigid gender roles and promoting positive representations of masculinity that celebrate diversity and authenticity. By challenging traditional notions of masculinity and encouraging men to embrace their full range of emotions and experiences, we can create a more inclusive and supportive society for everyone. By addressing toxic masculinity at its root, we can work towards building a more just and equitable world for all individuals, regardless of gender.

Unpacking Emotional Conflict

In the intricacies of masculinity lies a labyrinth of emotional conflict, a labyrinth that often envelopes men in a shroud of silence and solitude. From a young age, boys are taught to suppress emotions deemed as "weakness" - fear, sadness, vulnerability, or doubt. This suppression becomes a shield, protecting them from the scrutiny of a society that dictates stoicism and strength as essential components of masculinity.

However, this shield is not impenetrable. Beneath the surface of this carefully constructed facade, a battleground of emotions rages on. The unshed tears of loss, the unspoken words of longing, the hidden wounds of rejection - each one a piece of the fractured soul that lies buried deep within.

As men navigate the tumultuous waters of life, these unresolved emotional conflicts manifest in various ways. The weight of unexpressed emotions can morph into anxiety, enveloping them in a cloud of doubt and worry. The burden of unshed tears can lead to depression, casting a shadow on their days and nights. The ache of unspoken words can fester into anger, erupting like a volcano and scorching everything in its path.

Yet, amidst this chaos, there is a glimmer of hope. A chance for men to break free from the shackles of emotional suppression and embrace vulnerability as a source of strength and resilience. It is in the acceptance of one's own vulnerabilities that true courage resides, for it takes immense bravery to face the demons within and emerge stronger on the other side.

Through introspection and self-reflection, men can begin to unravel the tangled knots of their emotional conflicts. Therapy, support groups, or simply honest conversations with trusted individuals can serve as guiding lights on the path to healing. By allowing themselves to feel and express a full range of emotions, men can free themselves from the suffocating grip of toxic masculinity and redefine what it means to be strong, compassionate, and whole.

In this journey of self-discovery, men can discover the power of empathy, the beauty of connection, and the healing force of authenticity. By embracing their emotional landscapes with open hearts and open minds, they can pave the way for a new era of masculinity - one that celebrates vulnerability, nurtures emotional intelligence, and honors the depth and complexity of the human experience.

Healing Shame and Inadequacy

In this section, we explore the intricate layers of shame and inadequacy that permeate the lives of men, delving deeper into the complexities of their emotional struggles and the societal constructs that contribute to these challenges. The pervasive influence of traditional masculine norms fosters a culture of emotional suppression and performance-based self-worth, leaving many men wrestling with deep-seated feelings of shame and inadequacy that can be challenging to overcome.

From an early age, boys are taught to internalize the idea that vulnerability is synonymous with weakness, perpetuating a cycle of emotional suppression and disconnection from their authentic selves. This societal pressure to conform to rigid standards of masculinity creates a breeding ground for shame, as men constantly strive to live up to unattainable ideals of strength, invulnerability, and success.

The roots of shame often lie in childhood experiences of neglect, rejection, or emotional invalidation, reinforcing a narrative of unworthiness that becomes ingrained in the psyche. As men mature, this sense of inadequacy can manifest in destructive behaviors and coping mechanisms, such as aggression, substance abuse, or relationship challenges, as they seek to numb the pain of their inner turmoil.

Breaking free from the grip of shame requires a courageous willingness to confront one's vulnerabilities and embrace a more compassionate and authentic sense of self. Through introspection, therapy, and open dialogue with supportive individuals, men can begin to unravel the layers of conditioning that have shaped their self-perception and cultivate a more nurturing relationship with their emotions.

By challenging societal expectations and embracing a broader spectrum of masculinity that values emotional honesty and connection, men can embark on a journey of self-discovery and healing. This process of self-acceptance and growth requires patience and commitment, but offers a profound opportunity for men to reclaim their sense of self-worth and forge deeper connections with themselves and others.

In embracing vulnerability as a source of strength rather than weakness, men can transform their relationship with shame and inadequacy, paving the way for greater emotional resilience, authenticity, and fulfillment in their lives. Through this journey of self-exploration and healing, men can rewrite the narrative of their masculinity and embark on a path towards greater self-awareness and emotional well-being.

Embracing Vulnerability and Emotional Intelligence

In exploring the intricate relationship between vulnerability, emotional intelligence, and authentic masculinity, it is essential to delve deeper into the nuances of these interconnected concepts and their impact on men's lives. The societal conditioning that shapes men's expressions of emotion and vulnerability is rooted in age-old expectations of stoicism, self-reliance, and emotional detachment. These expectations often discourage men from embracing vulnerability as a sign of weakness, perpetuating a culture that values bravado over authenticity and emotional honesty.

The concept of emotional intelligence plays a pivotal role in shaping men's capacity to navigate their internal landscape and connect with others in meaningful ways. Emotional intelligence encompasses the ability to recognize, understand, and manage one's emotions effectively, as well as the capacity to empathize with others and communicate emotions in a healthy manner. Cultivating emotional intelligence requires men to engage in introspection, self-awareness, and empathy-building practices that foster a deeper understanding of their own emotions and those of others.

Toxic masculinity, characterized by traits such as aggression, dominance, and emotional suppression, poses significant challenges to men's mental health and well-being. The pressure to conform to these toxic norms can lead to a sense of disconnection from one's authentic self, as well as internalized shame and self-doubt. By perpetuating a narrow and rigid definition of masculinity, toxic norms limit men's emotional expression, stifling their ability to form genuine connections and engage in vulnerable, intimate relationships.

In challenging toxic masculinity and embracing vulnerability as a source of strength, men have the opportunity to redefine masculinity in more expansive and inclusive terms. Embracing vulnerability involves acknowledging one's imperfections, fears, and insecurities with courage and self-compassion, rather than hiding behind a facade of false strength. By embracing vulnerability as a pathway to deeper self-awareness and interpersonal connection, men can cultivate a more authentic and resilient sense of masculinity that honors their emotional complexity and capacity for growth.

Practical strategies for developing emotional intelligence and embracing vulnerability include engaging in mindfulness practices, seeking therapy or support groups, journaling about emotions, and engaging in open and honest communication with trusted individuals. By prioritizing emotional well-being and cultivating a greater sense of self-acceptance, men can begin to dismantle the barriers of toxic masculinity and embrace a more empowered and authentic experience of masculinity that honors their emotional truth and fosters genuine connection with themselves and others.

Building Healthy Relationships

In the intricate web of human connections, this section on building healthy relationships delves into the multifaceted dynamics that underlie our interactions with others. A cornerstone of healthy relationships is effective communication, which involves not only expressing oneself but also actively listening to and understanding the perspectives of others. Through open and honest dialogue, individuals can foster trust, empathy, and mutual respect, thus strengthening the foundation of their relationships.

Empathy, the ability to put oneself in another's shoes and understand their emotions, plays a pivotal role in building healthy relationships. By empathizing with others, individuals can bridge the gap between differing viewpoints, cultivate compassion, and forge deeper connections based on understanding and care. Empathy also allows for improved conflict resolution, as it encourages individuals to approach disagreements with a mindset of collaboration and compromise rather than defensiveness or hostility.

Setting boundaries is another crucial aspect of maintaining healthy relationships. Boundaries help individuals define their personal limits and protect their well-being by establishing clear guidelines for acceptable behavior within the relationship. By communicating boundaries openly and respectfully, individuals can foster a sense of safety and autonomy within their connections while also promoting mutual understanding and respect.

Resolving conflicts is an inevitable part of any relationship, but how conflicts are addressed can significantly impact the relationship's health and longevity. Healthy conflict resolution involves active listening, acknowledging each other's perspectives, and working together to find mutually agreeable solutions. By approaching conflicts with empathy, patience, and a willingness to compromise, individuals can navigate disagreements constructively and strengthen their bond through shared challenges.

Trust is the bedrock of healthy relationships, built on a foundation of honesty, reliability, and consistency. Trust is not easily earned but can be quickly shattered by dishonesty, betrayal, or inconsistency. Cultivating trust requires transparency, integrity, and a commitment to honoring one's word and actions. By demonstrating trustworthiness and reliability in their interactions, individuals can nurture a sense of security and intimacy in their relationships, fostering deeper connections and resilience in the face of adversity.

Lastly, it is essential to recognize the importance of self-care in the context of building healthy relationships. Individuals must prioritize their own well-being, set boundaries around their time and energy, and engage in activities that bring them joy and fulfillment. By taking care of oneself, individuals can show up as their best selves in their relationships, demonstrating self-respect, self-awareness, and emotional resilience.

In conclusion, building healthy relationships is a multifaceted journey that revolves around effective communication, empathy, boundaries, conflict resolution, trust, and self-care. By embracing these principles and committing to ongoing growth and learning within their relationships, individuals can cultivate connections that are authentic, supportive, and enriching, bringing greater meaning and fulfillment to their lives.

Empowering Men to Thrive

In this section, I explore the intricate interplay between societal expectations and toxic masculinity, delving into the nuanced ways in which these constructs shape men's experiences and well-being. The pressure to conform to rigid gender norms can have profound implications for men, constraining their ability to express vulnerability, seek help, and cultivate authentic connections with others.

One key aspect of toxic masculinity is the myth of emotional invulnerability, where men are often expected to suppress their emotions and present a façade of strength and stoicism. This expectation not only burdens men with the weight of shouldering their struggles alone but also perpetuates a culture of silence around mental health issues.

Studies have shown that men are less likely to seek professional help for mental health concerns compared to women, with factors such as stigma, fear of judgment, and internalized beliefs about masculinity playing a significant role in this disparity. Addressing these barriers and encouraging men to prioritize their emotional well-being is crucial in fostering a society where men feel empowered to seek help without shame or judgment.

Moreover, the impact of toxic masculinity extends beyond individual well-being to also affect relationships and communities. When men are socialized to prioritize aggression and dominance over emotional intelligence and empathy, it can lead to interpersonal conflicts, strained relationships, and a lack of emotional intimacy. By challenging these harmful ideologies and promoting healthier models of masculinity, we can cultivate more meaningful and fulfilling connections among individuals of all genders.

Redefining success for men involves embracing a broader understanding of achievement that goes beyond traditional markers of success. True success encompasses not just external accolades but also inner growth, emotional resilience, and the ability to foster genuine connections with others. By dismantling harmful stereotypes and cultivating a culture of authenticity and vulnerability, men can navigate their lives with a greater sense of purpose and fulfillment.

Ultimately, creating a more equitable and inclusive society requires us to recognize and challenge the harmful effects of toxic masculinity on men's mental health and overall well-being. By fostering empathy, understanding, and open dialogue around these issues, we can create a more compassionate world where individuals of all genders are supported in their journey towards holistic health and fulfillment.

The Future of Masculinity

In this section, I delve into the evolving landscape of masculinity in our modern society. As gender roles continue to shift and societal expectations change, the concept of masculinity is also undergoing a transformation. The traditional ideals of masculinity, rooted in notions of strength, stoicism, and dominance, are being challenged and redefined in the face of a more diverse and inclusive world.

Men today are navigating a complex and rapidly changing social environment that demands a more nuanced understanding of what it means to be a man. The pressure to adhere to traditional gender norms can be stifling, contributing to a range of issues including mental health struggles, relationship difficulties, and limited emotional expression. The expectations placed on men to conform to rigid stereotypes of masculinity can create a sense of isolation and disconnect from their true selves.

Toxic masculinity, a harmful ideology that prioritizes aggression, power, and control over empathy and vulnerability, continues to exert a damaging influence on individuals and society at large. The perpetuation of toxic masculinity can lead to harmful behaviors such as violence, misogyny, and discrimination. It is imperative for men to challenge and unlearn these toxic traits in order to foster healthier relationships and promote a more equitable and compassionate society.

Men have a crucial role to play in advancing gender equality and dismantling systems of oppression. By actively engaging in conversations about privilege, power dynamics, and intersectionality, men can become strong allies in the fight for a more just and inclusive world. Through introspection, education, and advocacy, men can work towards breaking down barriers to equality and creating spaces where all individuals feel valued and respected.

Embracing a more expansive and inclusive definition of masculinity that celebrates qualities such as compassion, empathy, and authenticity is vital for the well-being of individuals and society as a whole. By encouraging men to embrace their full range of emotions, nurture meaningful connections, and challenge harmful societal norms, we can pave the way for a future where masculinity is defined by authenticity and respect rather than by outdated stereotypes and expectations. It is through this collective effort that we can create a world where all individuals, regardless of gender, are free to express themselves fully and authentically.

"I found that with depression, one of the most important things you could realize is that you're not alone. You're not the first to go through it; you're not going to be the last to go through it."
— Dwayne "The Rock" Johnson

CHAPTER 4

Emotional Healing and Transformation

Embracing Vulnerability: The Power of Saying "I Need Help"

In a society that often values stoicism and self-reliance, admitting vulnerability and the need for help can be seen as a sign of weakness. However, in reality, embracing vulnerability takes incredible strength and courage.

Acknowledging our own limitations and reaching out for support when we need it is a powerful act of self-care and self-awareness. It requires humility, honesty, and a willingness to let go of the facade of invincibility.

Saying "I need help" can be a transformative moment in our lives. It opens the door to connection, healing, and growth. It allows us to release the burden of trying to do everything on our own and invites others to support us in our journey.

By embracing vulnerability and being willing to ask for help, we not only show ourselves compassion but also give permission for others to do the same. We create a space for authentic connections and deep relationships to flourish.

Vulnerability is not a sign of weakness; it is a testament to our humanity. It is in our moments of vulnerability that we show our true selves, stripped of pretense and bravado. It is in these moments that we allow others to see us for who we truly are, and in turn, invite them to do the same.

When we open ourselves up to vulnerability, we give ourselves the gift of growth and self-discovery. We learn to lean on others, to share our burdens, and to trust in the kindness and compassion of those around us. By embracing vulnerability, we create space for empathy, connection, and understanding to thrive.

Vulnerability is a gateway to authentic living. It is through our moments of vulnerability that we can truly connect with others on a deeper level. It allows us to break down walls and barriers, fostering genuine relationships based on openness and trust.

When we embrace vulnerability, we not only show strength in our willingness to be real and raw with others, but we also give them permission to do the same. We create a safe space for mutual support, understanding, and growth.

In asking for help, we demonstrate humility and a recognition of our interconnectedness. We acknowledge that we are not meant to navigate life's challenges alone, and that seeking assistance is a brave and wise choice.

So, the next time you find yourself in need of help, don't hesitate to speak up and say, "I need help." Embrace the power of vulnerability and trust that doing so is not a sign of weakness, but an affirmation of your strength and resilience.

Breaking Free from Cultural Conditioning: Embracing Emotions as Strength

Embracing emotions as strength is a profound journey of self-discovery and growth that transcends traditional notions of masculinity. In a society that often places a premium on stoicism and emotional suppression, men face unique challenges in allowing themselves to be vulnerable and authentic in their emotional expression.

The pressure to conform to rigid gender norms can create a barrier to true connection with oneself and others. Many men may struggle with feelings of shame or inadequacy when they experience emotions that are deemed as "weak" or "unmanly" by societal standards. This internalized stigma can prevent them from fully engaging with their emotional lives and hinder their ability to cultivate meaningful relationships.

However, the act of embracing emotions as strength is a revolutionary act of self-love and liberation. It involves letting go of outdated ideas about what it means to be a man and instead embracing a more holistic and compassionate understanding of masculinity. By honoring their emotional experiences and allowing themselves to be vulnerable, men can tap into a wellspring of resilience and courage that empowers them to navigate life's challenges with authenticity and grace.

Furthermore, embracing emotions as strength can have far-reaching positive effects on mental health and well-being. Research shows that individuals who are able to acknowledge and process their emotions in a healthy way are more likely to experience lower levels of anxiety, depression, and stress. By prioritizing emotional honesty and self-compassion, men can build a solid foundation for their overall psychological health and enhance their capacity for meaningful connections with others.

In essence, embracing emotions as strength is a radical act of self-empowerment and self-acceptance. It is a powerful declaration of one's humanity and a courageous step towards living a life that is aligned with one's true self. By embracing emotions as an essential part of the human experience, men can unlock a deeper sense of authenticity, connection, and fulfillment in their lives.

Moreover, this shift in perspective towards emotions can also lead to increased emotional intelligence. Men who allow themselves to embrace their emotions as strength are better equipped to understand and manage their own feelings as well as empathize with the emotions of others. This heightened emotional awareness can improve communication, foster healthier relationships, and contribute to a more compassionate and emotionally connected society at large.

By challenging the status quo and redefining masculinity to include emotional vulnerability and strength, men pave the way for a more inclusive and empathetic world where individuals are encouraged to embrace their full range of emotions without fear of judgment or stigma. This evolution in thinking not only benefits men personally but also contributes to the larger societal shift towards a more authentic and compassionate understanding of what it means to be human.

The Journey of Self-Discovery: Understanding and Expressing Feelings

In this section, we embark on a profound journey of self-discovery through the intricate tapestry of our emotional landscape. As we delve deep into the reservoir of our feelings, we unravel the intricate web of experiences and memories that have shaped the contours of our inner world.

Exploring the labyrinth of emotions, we confront the paradoxical nature of our human condition - the coexistence of joy and sorrow, love and fear, hope and despair. Our emotions serve as a visceral compass, guiding us through the labyrinth of our inner world, offering insights into the depths of our psyche and the essence of our being.

Amidst the turbulent waters of emotional turmoil, we find refuge in the sanctuary of self-awareness and mindfulness. By observing our feelings with gentle curiosity and compassion, we learn to untangle the knots of our emotional responses, peeling back the layers of conditioning and societal expectations that obscure our authentic selves.

Through the practice of radical acceptance and deep listening, we create a space for our feelings to unfold and reveal their hidden truths. Each emotion carries a message, a gift waiting to be unwrapped with reverence and humility. By embracing our emotional landscape with an open heart and a willing spirit, we deepen our connection to the inner wisdom that resides within each feeling.

In the alchemy of emotional expression, we discover the transformative power of vulnerability and authenticity. Our emotions are not to be feared or suppressed but rather celebrated as an integral part of our human experience. When we honor our feelings with courage and compassion, we open ourselves to the transformative potential of emotional healing and growth.

As we navigate the intricate dance of emotions, let us remember that each feeling is a portal to self-discovery and self-love. By cultivating a sense of curiosity and openness towards our emotional landscape, we invite a deeper understanding of ourselves and pave the way for profound growth and transformation. Embrace your emotions as sacred messengers of truth, guiding you on your journey towards wholeness and authenticity.

Overcoming Shame and Stigma: The Evolution of Masculinity

In a society where traditional notions of masculinity have often been tied to stoicism and emotional suppression, many men have faced the challenge of overcoming shame and stigma in order to embrace a more authentic and holistic version of themselves.

The evolution of masculinity is an ongoing journey that requires introspection, vulnerability, and a willingness to challenge societal norms. This process often involves confronting deep-seated beliefs and narratives about what it means to be a man, and shedding light on the harmful impact of toxic masculinity on both individuals and communities.

Men are often conditioned from a young age to adhere to strict gender norms that dictate how they should express themselves emotionally. This can lead to a sense of shame and internalized stigma around vulnerability, as any deviation from the traditional masculine script is often met with ridicule or dismissal. As a result, many men learn to bury their feelings, leading to a disconnect from their authentic selves and a cycle of emotional suppression.

The journey towards redefining masculinity involves breaking free from these constraints and allowing oneself to be fully seen and heard. It requires men to navigate the complexities of their emotions, confront their insecurities, and cultivate a deeper sense of self-awareness. This process is not easy, as it often involves unraveling years of conditioning and unlearning harmful behaviors that have been ingrained over time.

By acknowledging and addressing feelings of shame and stigma surrounding emotions and mental health, men can begin to redefine masculinity in a way that is more inclusive and compassionate. This includes challenging stereotypes that perpetuate the idea that vulnerability is a sign of weakness, and instead recognizing it as a strength that allows for deeper connections and personal growth.

Through open conversations, support networks, and self-reflection, men can break free from the confines of traditional masculinity and embrace a more authentic and empowered sense of self. By sharing their experiences and supporting one another in this journey, men can create a culture that celebrates emotional intelligence, empathy, and genuine connection.

The evolution of masculinity is a transformative process that has the power to not only benefit individual men, but also to contribute to a more equitable and harmonious society. It is a journey of self-discovery, healing, and empowerment that requires courage and resilience, but ultimately leads to a more fulfilling and meaningful way of being in the world.

As men continue to explore and redefine their identities, it is important to recognize the intersections of gender, race, sexuality, and other aspects of identity that influence how masculinity is experienced and expressed. This intersectional approach allows for a more nuanced understanding of the diverse ways in which men navigate their gender identity and challenges the idea of a monolithic concept of masculinity.

In order to create a more inclusive and supportive environment for men to explore and redefine masculinity, it is crucial to address the systemic barriers and social norms that perpetuate harmful ideals of what it means to be a man. This includes challenging harmful behaviors such as aggression, dominance, and emotional suppression, and instead promoting values of empathy, vulnerability, and emotional literacy.

By engaging in this ongoing dialogue and collective effort to redefine masculinity, men can not only liberate themselves from the constraints of toxic masculinity but also contribute to a more compassionate and socially just world for all individuals, regardless of gender identity. It is through this dedication to growth, self-awareness, and empathy that men can truly transform the landscape of masculinity for future generations.

Healing from Trauma: Reclaiming Your Emotional Well-being

In this section, we delve deeper into the intricate journey of healing from trauma and reclaiming emotional well-being. Trauma, in its various forms, can leave lasting scars on a person's psyche, impacting their mental health and emotional stability. Men, in particular, may struggle to address and overcome past traumas due to societal expectations around masculinity and emotional expression.

Reclaiming emotional well-being requires a profound commitment to self-exploration and healing. It involves delving into the depths of one's emotional landscape, navigating the turbulent waters of past pain, and gradually finding a path towards inner peace and wholeness.

Acknowledging past traumas and their impact is a crucial first step in this healing journey. It requires courage to face the memories and emotions that have long been buried or suppressed. By bravely confronting these experiences, men can begin to unravel the tangled knots of their past and move towards a place of acceptance and healing.

Therapy, both individual and group, can serve as a vital tool in this process. A skilled therapist can offer guidance, support, and a safe space for men to explore their innermost thoughts and feelings. Through therapy, men can learn coping mechanisms, gain insights into their patterns of behavior, and begin the transformative work of healing.

Self-care practices are also integral to the journey of reclaiming emotional well-being. Engaging in activities that nourish the mind, body, and spirit can help men cultivate resilience and strengthen their emotional foundation. Mindfulness practices, such as meditation and deep breathing, can assist in soothing the nervous system and fostering a sense of inner calm.

Moreover, physical exercise, creative expression, and time spent in nature can all contribute to a sense of wholeness and well-being. By prioritizing self-care and committing to practices that promote emotional healing, men can begin to reestablish a sense of equilibrium and connection to themselves.

It's essential for men to recognize that the healing process is not a linear trajectory. Setbacks, triggers, and moments of intense emotion are all natural components of healing from trauma. Patience, self-compassion, and a willingness to seek support during challenging times are crucial elements in this journey toward emotional well-being.

By courageously confronting past traumas, actively engaging in self-care practices, and seeking support when needed, men can gradually reclaim their emotional well-being and experience a profound sense of empowerment and renewal. Healing is a journey that requires dedication and perseverance, but the rewards of inner peace and emotional freedom are immeasurable.

The journey towards reclaiming emotional well-being also involves exploring the various aspects of masculinity that may have influenced how a man navigates through trauma. Societal norms around masculinity can often limit emotional expression and vulnerability, creating barriers to healing. By challenging these ingrained beliefs and embracing a more holistic view of manhood, men can create space for deeper emotional exploration and healing.

Cultural stereotypes and societal pressures can greatly impact a man's ability to seek help and support for his emotional struggles. The stigma surrounding mental health issues and the expectation for men to always remain strong and stoic can create barriers to accessing essential resources for healing. Breaking free from these constraints requires a willingness to challenge outdated notions of masculinity and prioritize one's emotional well-being above societal expectations.

In addition to therapy and self-care practices, building strong social connections and support networks can be instrumental in the healing process. Opening up to trusted friends, family members, or support groups can offer a sense of validation, understanding, and encouragement as men navigate through their healing journey. Creating a sense of community and belonging can provide a vital source of strength and solidarity during challenging times.

Furthermore, engaging in activities that promote self-discovery and personal growth can help men uncover new facets of themselves and redefine their sense of identity beyond their past traumas. Exploring hobbies, interests, and creative outlets can stimulate a sense of purpose and fulfillment, fostering a renewed sense of agency and control over one's narrative.

As men journey through the process of healing from trauma and reclaiming emotional well-being, it's important to remember that vulnerability is not a sign of weakness but a courageous step towards self-discovery and growth. Embracing one's emotions, seeking support when needed, and committing to self-compassion are essential components in building a strong foundation for emotional well-being. By embarking on this profound journey of healing, men can cultivate resilience, inner strength, and a deep sense of authenticity that allows them to reclaim their emotional well-being with grace and empowerment.

The Importance of Men's Groups: Building Brotherhood and Support

In the realm of men's groups, a profound shift is taking place—a movement towards redefining masculinity and creating spaces for authentic connection, vulnerability, and personal growth. Within the walls of these gatherings, men are reclaiming their emotional selves, challenging societal expectations, and forging deep bonds built on trust and mutual support.

One of the central pillars of men's groups is the emphasis on emotional expression and vulnerability. Historically, men have been conditioned to repress their feelings, uphold a facade of strength, and avoid showing any perceived weakness. However, within the container of a men's group, these norms are dismantled, and a new paradigm emerges—one in which emotional openness is not only accepted but celebrated. By sharing their innermost thoughts, fears, and struggles, men in these groups cultivate a sense of authenticity and connection that is transformative.

Beyond the individual healing that occurs within men's groups, there is also a collective power at play. Through shared experiences, group discussions, and collaborative activities, members form a brotherhood that transcends traditional notions of friendship. This camaraderie creates a sense of belonging and solidarity that is deeply nourishing and affirming. In a world where men are often isolated and compartmentalized, these groups provide a sense of community and belonging that is essential for holistic well-being.

Moreover, men's groups play a vital role in challenging toxic masculinity and promoting healthy masculinity. By confronting rigid gender roles, encouraging empathy and emotional intelligence, and fostering respectful communication, these groups are at the forefront of a cultural shift towards a more expansive and inclusive understanding of what it means to be a man. In embracing vulnerability and authenticity, members of men's groups not only transform themselves but also contribute to a broader movement towards positive masculinity that benefits individuals and society as a whole.

In essence, men's groups offer a sacred space where men can explore, heal, and grow in the company of like-minded individuals. Through the power of shared experience, mutual support, and collective transformation, these groups are not only changing the lives of their members but also reshaping the landscape of masculinity in a profound and meaningful way.

Furthermore, the impact of men's groups extends beyond the confines of their meetings. Members often bring the insights and practices learned in group settings into their daily lives, resulting in healthier relationships, increased emotional intelligence, and a greater sense of purpose. By embodying the values of vulnerability, empathy, and authenticity, men become agents of positive change in their communities and beyond.

As men continue to explore the depths of their emotional selves and challenge traditional norms of masculinity, the ripple effects of this movement are felt far and wide. From fostering greater understanding between the genders to dismantling harmful stereotypes and fostering social change, men's groups have the potential to reshape the fabric of society by nurturing a new generation of emotionally intelligent, empathetic, and authentic men.

Transformative Experiences: The New Warrior Training Adventure

In addition to the experiential exercises and emotional healing processes found within the New Warrior Training Adventure, participants also engage in deep introspection and reflection to uncover and address long-standing patterns and limiting beliefs that have held them back in their lives. Through guided meditations, journaling exercises, and one-on-one conversations with facilitators, men are encouraged to explore the root causes of their behaviors and thought patterns, gaining valuable insights into their subconscious motivations and desires.

One of the central themes of the training adventure is the concept of the "Hero's Journey," a narrative framework that mirrors the universal pattern of personal growth and transformation found in myths and legends throughout human history. Participants are invited to see themselves as the hero of their own story, embarking on a journey of self-discovery, facing challenges and obstacles, and ultimately emerging stronger and more empowered on the other side.

The inner work done during the training adventure often involves confronting deep-seated fears, unresolved traumas, and unexpressed emotions that have been buried beneath layers of societal conditioning and personal armor. By creating a safe and supportive environment for men to explore these sensitive and vulnerable aspects of themselves, the training adventure offers a unique opportunity for healing and growth that is both profound and transformative.

The concept of masculinity is also explored in depth during the training adventure, challenging traditional notions of what it means to be a man in today's society. Men are encouraged to embrace a more holistic and flexible understanding of masculinity, one that allows for vulnerability, emotional expression, and authentic connection with others. By breaking free from stereotypes and societal expectations, participants are able to cultivate a more authentic and fulfilling sense of self, grounded in their own values, beliefs, and passions.

Through the combination of experiential exercises, emotional healing processes, deep introspection, and redefinition of masculinity, the New Warrior Training Adventure offers men a profound opportunity to peel back the layers of conditioning that have kept them from fully expressing themselves and connecting with others. It is a journey of self-discovery and personal growth that invites men to embrace all facets of their being, both light and shadow, and to step into their true power and potential with courage, compassion, and authenticity.

The Role of Men's Coaches in Emotional Healing and Transformation

Men's coaches play a profoundly impactful role in guiding men through the complex and often challenging journey of emotional healing and transformation. In a world where traditional masculinity can sometimes limit the expression and exploration of emotions, these coaches provide a safe and nurturing space for men to delve into their innermost thoughts and feelings.

By fostering an environment of trust and empathy, men's coaches create a platform for men to confront their vulnerabilities, confront their fears, and break through self-imposed barriers. Through insightful conversations, reflective exercises, and personalized guidance, these professionals help men uncover the layers of conditioning and societal expectations that may have hindered their emotional growth.

One of the key aspects of men's coaching is encouraging men to embrace their emotions and develop a deeper understanding of themselves. This involves cultivating emotional intelligence, learning to identify and express feelings in a healthy way, and building resilience in the face of life's challenges.

Men's coaches also play a pivotal role in supporting men as they navigate through past traumas, limiting beliefs, or patterns of behavior that no longer serve them. By addressing these underlying issues with compassion and skillful guidance, men's coaches help their clients pave the way for healing, growth, and personal transformation.

Furthermore, men's coaches empower men to cultivate more meaningful and fulfilling relationships, both with themselves and others. Through coaching sessions focused on communication skills, boundary setting, and self-discovery, men learn how to show up authentically, connect deeply with others, and create healthier dynamics in their personal and professional lives.

In essence, men's coaches serve as allies and mentors in the journey towards emotional well-being and self-actualization. By providing a supportive and encouraging presence, these coaches enable men to embrace their vulnerabilities, tap into their inherent strength, and live authentically in alignment with their true selves.

Additionally, men's coaches often help men explore the intersection of masculinity and mental health, challenging societal norms that may perpetuate toxic behaviors and attitudes. By encouraging men to break free from traditional stereotypes of stoicism and toughness, these coaches create space for vulnerability and emotional expression, fostering a more holistic and authentic connection to self and others.

Moreover, men's coaches may incorporate mindfulness practices, somatic experiencing techniques, and other therapeutic modalities to help men cultivate a deeper sense of self-awareness and presence. By integrating mind-body approaches into coaching sessions, men can learn to regulate their emotions, manage stress more effectively, and cultivate a greater sense of inner harmony and peace.

In this way, men's coaches play an essential role in guiding men towards a more meaningful and fulfilling life, empowering them to embrace their emotions, cultivate deeper connections, and step into their fullest potential as compassionate, authentic, and resilient individuals.

Navigating Mental Health: Resources and Support for Men

Navigating Mental Health: Resources and Support for Men

Navigating mental health challenges can be a complex and deeply personal journey, particularly for men who often face societal pressures to uphold a facade of strength and stoicism. However, it is crucial to recognize that seeking help and support is vital for maintaining emotional well-being and fostering resilience. Here are some comprehensive resources and strategies to support men in their mental health journey:

1. Therapy and Counseling: The benefits of therapy and counseling cannot be overstated in the realm of mental health support. Working with a skilled therapist provides a safe and confidential

space to unpack and process emotions, explore underlying issues, and learn effective coping mechanisms. Therapists can offer specialized treatments for various mental health conditions,
such as cognitive-behavioral therapy (CBT) for anxiety and depression, trauma-focused therapy for PTSD, and interpersonal
therapy for relationship issues. It is essential for men to overcome any stigma or reluctance to seek therapy and recognize it
as a proactive step towards emotional well-being.

2.   Support Groups: Men's support groups and mental health sup-
     port groups offer a unique opportunity for men to connect with
     others who share similar experiences and challenges. Participat-
     ing in a support group can help combat feelings of isolation, fos-
     ter a sense of camaraderie, and provide a platform for sharing
     and learning from one another. These groups can be in-person
     or virtual, offering flexibility in accessing support. Being part of
     a supportive community can help men feel understood, validat-
     ed, and encouraged to take positive steps towards better mental
     health.

3.   Hotlines and Helplines: In times of acute distress or crisis, ho-
     tlines and helplines are crucial resources for immediate emo-
     tional support and intervention. Trained professionals are avail-
     able to listen, offer guidance, and connect individuals with ap-
     propriate resources. Services like the National Suicide Preven-
     tion Lifeline, Crisis Text Line, and local helplines can provide
     a lifeline for individuals in urgent need of assistance. It is im-
     portant for men to recognize that reaching out for help during a
     crisis is a sign of strength, not weakness.

4.   Online Resources: The digital landscape has opened up a world
     of mental health resources at our fingertips. Websites, online fo-
     rums, and social media platforms are valuable sources of infor-
     mation, self-help tools, and virtual communities where individ-

uals can find support and solidarity. Online therapy services and mental health apps also offer convenient avenues for accessing counseling and self-care tools. Men can utilize these resources to learn more about mental health, find coping strategies, and connect with others who are on a similar journey.

5. Self-Care Practices: Self-care is an essential aspect of maintaining mental well-being. Engaging in regular exercise, prioritizing nutritious meals, practicing mindfulness and relaxation techniques, and ensuring adequate sleep are fundamental self-care practices that support emotional resilience. Additionally, hobbies, creative outlets, and time spent in nature can nurture a sense of fulfillment and balance. Men should prioritize self-care as a daily habit to build resilience in the face of life's challenges.

6. Medication and Treatment: For some individuals, medication may be a necessary component of their mental health treatment plan. Consulting with a qualified healthcare provider, such as a psychiatrist or primary care physician, can help determine the appropriateness of medication and monitor its effectiveness. It is essential to follow medical advice and attend follow-up appointments for optimal management of mental health conditions. Men should approach medication as a tool that can work in conjunction with therapy and self-care practices to support their mental health.

7. Educating Yourself: Knowledge is a powerful tool in navigating mental health challenges. Empowering yourself with information about common mental health conditions, symptoms, treatment options, and self-care strategies equips you to make informed decisions about your well-being. Education also helps reduce stigma surrounding mental health issues and encourages open dialogue about emotional struggles. Men should actively

seek to educate themselves about mental health to better understand their own experiences and advocate for their well-being.

By embracing a holistic approach to mental health and actively seeking support, men can cultivate emotional resilience, nurture meaningful connections, and cultivate a greater sense of well-being. Remember, prioritizing your mental health is a courageous act that paves the way for a more enriched and fulfilling life. Embrace the support available to you and take proactive steps towards your well-being.

Building a Stronger, Healthier Future: Embracing Emotional, Intellectual, and Spiritual Growth

In the vast tapestry of human existence, the pursuit of growth and self-discovery stands as a sacred and transformative journey that we undertake with unwavering dedication and reverence. As we delve deeper into the intricate layers of our being, we unearth hidden reservoirs of wisdom, resilience, and compassion that shape the very essence of who we are and propel us towards a more profound understanding of our place in the interconnected web of life.

Emotional growth, the foundational pillar of our inner landscape, invites us to traverse the depths of our emotions with courage and authenticity. It beckons us to embrace our vulnerabilities, fears, and joys with open hearts and minds, cultivating a profound sense of self-awareness and empathy that enables us to forge deeper connections with ourselves and others. Through the alchemy of emotional intelligence, we learn to navigate the turbulent waters of our inner world with grace and resilience, weaving a tapestry of emotional richness that imbues our lives with meaning and purpose.

Intellectual growth, the guiding beacon of our cognitive prowess, propels us towards the boundless horizons of knowledge and innovation. It ignites the flames of curiosity within us, inspiring us to embark on a perpetual quest for learning, critical thinking, and intellectual discourse. As we immerse ourselves in the vast ocean of ideas and perspectives, we sharpen our analytical faculties, expand our creative horizons, and cultivate a deep wellspring of intellectual resilience that empowers us to unravel the mysteries of the universe and shape the course of our destinies with wisdom and insight.

Spiritual growth, the transcendent force that unites us with the divine essence of the cosmos, calls us to embark on a sacred pilgrimage of inner transformation and connection. It beckons us to delve into the sacred chambers of our souls, where the eternal flame of our spirit burns brightly, illuminating the path towards self-realization and enlightenment. By nurturing our spiritual essence and cultivating a sense of unity with all creation, we align ourselves with the cosmic rhythms of existence, attuning our hearts and minds to the harmonious flow of life and imbuing each moment with a deep sense of purpose, peace, and interconnectedness.

As we weave together the intricate threads of emotional, intellectual, and spiritual growth, we create a tapestry of profound richness and depth that elevates our existence to new heights of self-awareness, transformation, and authenticity. In the radiant interplay of these fundamental components, we discover the true essence of who we are and unlock the boundless potential that resides within us, forging a path towards a brighter, more luminous future grounded in the radiant splendor of our evolving selves.

Stories of Transformation

One of the challenges men face when beginning their transformational journey is the belief that no one will understand their pain. I remember going to therapy and thinking no one could relate to all of the trauma I had gone through. After being involved with men's work, I've learned that most men can definitely relate to my pain because they too had

experienced their own pain. Pain transcends, race, religion, age, or social economic status, pain is pain, and as men, we all experience different levels of it. When I began my healing journey, I came across a quote
that gave me the courage to go to therapy in order to heal my pain.
It was a quote by a therapist named John Bradshaw whose work truly
changed my life. John said: "The only way to heal is to create an interpersonal bridge with another human being." After reading that quote, I
knew I needed to learn how to create the bridge he was talking about so
I went to therapy to learn how to create that bridge.

I have come to know that one of the most powerful ways to create
that bridge is to be willing to share our stories with others. When we
allow ourselves to be open and vulnerable with another human being,
healing occurs because it allows us to feel and heal and be witnessed by
another human being. That's the key to your healing. To be willing to
share your story, no matter how difficult or painful. This is the beauty
of vulnerability. When we surrender, and become willing to open our
hearts and share the parts of ourselves we thought were unlovable it
allows our hearts to heal and let go of all the pain we've been carrying
around.

I'd like to close this chapter with an article I wrote about my
experience with therapy and three stories from men who have been on
their transformational journey like I have. Our stories should let you
know that transformation is possible if you're willing to do your inner
work and transform your life from the inside out.

Coach Michael Taylor

Men's Emotional Healing

*In 1989, I was experiencing a series of traumatic experiences that were
beginning to take their toll. My divorce and separation from my kids
were extremely painful and had begun to negatively impact my life. I had*

slipped into a deep state of depression and was barely able to function on a daily basis. As my depression deepened I went into isolation in which I literally shut myself off from the outside world. Although I was able to go to work and function in that capacity, I was completely disconnected from any social settings. I was not dating. I did not socialize with my friends. I had difficulty sleeping. I would rarely eat, and I had began to lose weight, which was rare for me, being a former personal trainer who took excellent care of my physical body. After several months I began to have fleeting thoughts of suicide, and it appeared that my situation was hopeless.

In an effort to alleviate some of the pain, I begin to read books dealing with depression. As I read them I could see myself in some of the stories. I definitely had all of the symptoms of depression, and I knew that I had to deal with it head on if I ever wanted to get my life back on track. After reading several books I realized that I was still deeply depressed and had not really begun to deal with the issues that were causing my depression. Instinctively I knew that I needed help, and I decided that I would go to therapy.

After making the decision to get help, another series of challenges surfaced. First of all, how was I going to find a therapist? How would I know which one to choose? What if the therapist couldn't help me? Would I be able to change? Could therapy "fix" me? What about the money? I was completely broke and definitely could not pay someone to listen to my problems. What was I going to do? These are just a few of the questions that were going through my mind. My greatest fear was wondering what would happen if my employees found out. As a manager, I was considered the leader, and I definitely did not want to appear weak in front of my co-workers. I believed that I needed to keep this a secret so that I would not lose the respect of my employees. In addition, I did not want my superiors to know because I thought I might lose my job if they found out.

After a few months of agonizing over these questions I knew that I had to take the chance and try therapy. I didn't have any other choice. It was seek help or die. There was no grey area. I decided that I definitely wanted to live, and I somehow gained the courage to go to the therapist's office.

My first attempt at therapy did not go well. I walked into a therapist's office and pretended that I was seeking information for a friend. I'm sure the people there knew this, but they allowed me to walk out with some of their brochures and a phone number to their suicide hotline. To be honest, I was absolutely terrified. Although I was scared, deep down I knew that I would have to find the courage to try again. I waited a few days and tried a different therapist's office. This time I had a completely different result. As I walked into the office, I believe the receptionist picked up on my fear. I had begun asking her questions about depression and whether or not they had any books that I could read. All of a sudden a therapist walked out and began asking me questions. "May I help you?" she asked. "Not really, I'm just looking for a little information about depression." " Are you depressed?" "I'm not really sure," I answered. "Why don't you come inside, and let's talk a little. Is that all right?" "I guess so."

As I followed her into her office, it felt as if my heart was going to jump out of my chest. I was so nervous and afraid that I was literally dripping with sweat. She obviously picked up on this and began to put my mind at ease.

"What is your name?"

"Michael."

"Well, Michael, I can sense that you are a little nervous, so let me start by asking what I can do to help you. Is there anything I can do for you?"

"Well, maybe. I have been doing some research about depression, and I think I'm depressed, but I'm really not sure."

"Do you feel depressed?"

"Based on what I've read so far, I think I am. But to be completely honest I'm not sure I know exactly what depression is supposed to feel like. Does that make any sense to you?'

"It makes a lot of sense to me. Unfortunately most men do not recognize how they feel. Men have been conditioned to disconnect from their emotions, and that makes it extremely difficult for men to express how they really feel. Most men will tell you what they think, but they usually do not know how they feel. You apparently fit into this category."

"I'm not sure if I really understand what you are saying, but a part of me thinks that you are right."

"You just validated the point I made. You are currently speaking from an intellectual perspective instead of an emotional one. It sounds as if you are disconnected from your emotions."

"Lets assume that you are right. If I am disconnected from my emotions, how do I get reconnected? Do you have any books on how to do this?

"Unfortunately you can not reconnect to your emotions by reading books. In order for you to reconnect, you have to relearn how to feel. This can be accomplished through therapy with me or any trained therapist."

"I really don't understand what you mean. But if I decide to relearn how to feel, how long will it take?

"I really can't answer that question. It's really up to you and how committed you are to doing the work."

"What do you mean doing the work? What kind of work is involved?"

"In the therapeutic community, we use the word 'work' because it takes a considerable amount of effort to heal yourself so that you can reconnect with your emotions. Doing the work means that you become willing to opening yourself up on an emotional level. This can be quite difficult at times."

"Well, I believe I'm ready. I'm really tired of being alone, and I definitely want to experience some fun in my life again. I think I can do this, so how much will it cost?"

"I operate on a sliding scale based on your ability to pay. The most important thing is for you to make the commitment to yourself to heal, and we can address the money issue at a later date. Are you ready to begin? Let's set up a date and time for you to begin your healing."

"I just want to thank you for being so nice and understanding. The truth is, I was about to run out of your office before you showed up. Now I am really glad that I came because I really believe that you can help me."

"That is a great attitude to have. I'm glad that you trust me enough to work with you. Just remember that I can guide you, but you must be willing to do the work. As long as you believe that you can heal, I can assure you that you will. Just stay committed and trust the process, and you will be just fine. The truth is you have already done the hard part by showing up today. It takes an incredible amount of courage to be here, and I'm proud of you for taking the first step."

As I left the therapist's office that day I knew that I had just taken the biggest step of my life. I did not know what to expect, but I knew that I was willing to do whatever it took to heal my emotions and relearn how to feel. I became committed to my own healing, and I can now say that I am emotionally healed and connected to my authentic self. As the therapist mentioned, it was not easy, but it was definitely possible. It has been one of the most challenging yet most fulfilling journeys of my life. I can not put into words the joy I feel on a regular basis as a result of doing my emotional work. My relationships now work, my creativity and sense of reverence is enhanced, my love of nature has been rekindled, and my professional life is rewarding and fulfilling. I took the road less traveled, and it has made all the difference in the world for me.

I wanted to share this story because there is such a negative stigma about men and therapy, and I believe it's time for a new conversation. In this new conversation men will recognize the importance of healing their emotions, and they will put forth the effort to do their healing work. When we learn to support each other in our growth we can remove the fear and stigma of being emotionally vulnerable, which will ultimately result in us being happier human beings. I believe that this is the most important work in which men can participate, and we must begin supporting each other through this process. If we will gain the courage to do this work, we will see a decline in domestic violence, child abuse, alcoholism, and random acts of violence.

The time has come for a new conversation about our emotional healing. Are you willing to join the conversation?

Coach Michael Taylor
www.coachmichaeltaylor.com

Dwayne Klassen
Men's Coach and author

Transformation into The Remarkable Man

In every man's life, there are markers and checkpoints along the path to guide him in the direction he's meant to go. However, free will gives him the choice to either pay attention to the signs or ignore them. Additionally, it is his level of awareness that will dictate whether or not he even sees them.

The fact that you are reading this book indicates you already have the awareness. The question is, what choices are you making that support that awareness?

Over the next few minutes, I'd like to invite you to come with me on a profound journey of self-discovery to what I call "Becoming The Remarkable Man." Consider this chapter to be one of those signs on your own personal journey.

As The Coach For Remarkable Men for the last 13 years, I've had the honor and pleasure of working with countless amazing men and couples *from all walks of life. In that time period, I too, have grown so much that I hardly recognize the man I once was.*

A big part of my transformation was, in fact, a result of creating my Remarkable Man brand and then becoming the man I needed to be to fulfill that destiny. Yes, I put the cart before the horse.

I'd love to tell you I started a national men's group, wrote a best-selling book, and launched into coaching because I was being altruistic and following my calling, but that's only half the truth.

I did it because it was me that needed the help. It was me that desperately wanted to change my life, and it was me that knew I needed to be a better man. Everything I was teaching was exactly what I needed to hear. But the biggest piece of all was that it was me that needed a brotherhood.

I wanted my own band of brothers that had my back. In fact, that became our tagline, "I've got your back!"

It was in doing men's work that forced me to be a better man. I had to rise to the occasion and step boldly into the man I wanted to be. My brothers held me to a higher standard. And it was this higher standard that made all the difference. It is said that "A rising tide lifts all boats." Well, that's exactly what we did for one another. We lifted each other up to a new level of possibility.

But here's the rub, I was a terrible student of my own journey. I resisted my greatness at every turn. My ego was so in control, and I allowed my core wounds to drive the bus.

I knew intellectually what to do, and I could tell others what and how to do what needed to get done, but when it came to my own life, it seemed like I was locked out of my own greatness.

I felt so incongruent and unauthentic, and did not know how to shift out of it. Until one day, an inspiration came. "What if you just went into radical honesty? What if you just spoke your truth? You know, the stuff you've kept to yourself. What if you just told the men exactly how you feel? That very thing you want from them?

So I did. I spoke my truth about feeling not good enough, about having imposter syndrome running the organization, and struggling with the duality of what the world sees and what the truth actually is. It was in this moment that a turning point occurred. An epoch in time that became foundational for, not only me, but the men's group as a whole. The men leaned into what I was saying, and after I was done, they admitted that this was the first time that I truly had connected to their heart and soul as their leader. It was then that they affirmed my character, leadership, and the man I was BEING in the moment. It was the most authentic moment of my life.

The Remarkable Man Project soon exploded across western Canada. We began to impact the lives of more and more men, and the women that loved them. But more than that, it was the radical honesty, and the confidential, safe, no BS container men were craving so that they could get real with what was really going on in their lives.

Once you can get to the truth of your existence and how you are living, then you have a path to a solution and a desired outcome.

I share this with you because, even though our movement disbanded during the Covid years, the legacy of what was created lives on. Not only in the hundreds of men we served, but in me as a man personally. The radical honesty rule and the brotherhood was, and is, pivotal in my expansion and transformation of who I am to this day.

I want you to make sure that you make this chapter count. Where in your life could radical honesty serve your highest good? Is it in your relationship, career, money, health, or your well-being?

I know there's a lot coming to the surface right now in any or all areas, but the place I want you to start is with the man in the mirror.

In fact, after you read this chapter, I invite you to do this exercise:

Ideally, do this alone in the house if you can, or if you have a car do this there (there's a reason for this you'll understand).

Go to your bathroom or bedroom where you have a mirror. Take a few deep breaths and look into your own eyes. Look deep into your eyes until you actually see yourself. You'll know it when you do. Do not look away.

Then ask yourself, "If you were radically honest with me right now, what would you say to me?"

Keep asking until something comes up.

It may be right there and has been waiting a long time to be expressed, or you might feel resistance and uncomfortable. That's just the ego blocking you from letting go. Push past the resistance and engage fully.

A lot of energy and emotion could come up with this. Let it happen. That's why being in the car is ideal, as most vehicles are incredibly sound insulated. They are a safe and private place for a man to rage, vent, cry, and be free to express all his emotions without alarming (or scaring) family members.

Do this exercise fully until you get past the usual filters and discomfort, and really go all-in. Don't stop until you feel you've let it all go! There might be a lot of self-hate, rage, anger, sadness, and grief in the lies you've told yourself, so let it come up. Dump the heavy load, brother!

If you can get radically honest with yourself first, then you can get radically honest with those you care about most. Be mindful of the space you are in and who you are sharing with. Radical honesty does not give you license to shame, bully, scare, or belittle others. This is your honesty, so make it about you and your own ownership of your feelings and triggers.

The real truth, and your ability to stand in the fire with it, is the key to your salvation and transformation.

If you are in a men's group already, allow that container to truly serve you at the highest level by being in your truth with your brothers even if it's hard. Admit that it is, and you'll feel right at home.

Your truth will set you free.

You've got this! Be Remarkable!

Dwayne Klassen
The Coach For Remarkable Men

Wayne Dawson

The VIP Shift: From 40 to Manhood!

Approaching 40 was as challenging and scary as my teen years. I felt totally vulnerable, uncertain and afraid. During my 40th birthday party, I made my rounds to greet my guests. My friend, Neal (now deceased), played the keyboards in the background. My other buddy, Chaver, strummed a Marley tune accompanying Neal on the bass.

At some point in the evening, I canvassed the 20 or more guests, including neighbors, close friends, and relatives. The average age of my dinner party attendees must have been approximately 45 years old. This was my daunting realization: I had crossed the threshold into the "dreaded" midlife.

Midlife crisis is not imagined. It is frigging real!

During my 40s, I became preoccupied with the fear of getting old; of not putting aside enough money for my kids' college and my retirement; for feeling anxious about outgrowing my career of 15 years. I wanted to fire my bosses, and my relationship with my then-wife was lacking - we were more roommates than 'yoked" couple.

My midlife existence felt empty. I needed MORE. When I decided to cheat without much censor, I figured I was extending and recapturing my youthful vigor and was still able to "play in the Game!" By the time 44 hit, my midlife crisis had consumed me.

My Ex discovered that I had been cheating on her with a younger woman who was carrying my baby. My health suffered due to various stressors, and I was diagnosed with IBS (Irritable Bowel Syndrome).

After the breakup and the end to my formerly secure and matrimonial life, I faced head-on the consequences of my affair, having to move into my old college friend's basement apartment in the home of his parents. The conditions were horrendous; feces seeping up through the floor in the rear section of the basement; an empty refrigerator most days. I struggled psychologically to adjust to living conditions away from my children and our beautiful home. The shame I brought onto my family due to my licentious behavior and my dire financial status, having to support three homes rather than one, eventually took its toll.

I went back to school, only this time as an Adjunct Professor, juggling to stay afloat. The demands and stress were burning me out.

I eventually got fired from my full-time career position. When you're in an executive position, the firing can be quite a production. They called me into the Headquarters on a Wednesday morning. Vito, my Italian American Division Director, invited me into his office. I had grown accustomed to meeting with my boss over the years but this time it was different. He remained standing and didn't offer me a seat. Then Michael, the Head of Youth Services, followed behind and closed the door.

There had been somewhat of an unspoken "power struggle" between Michael and me ever since we met years ago in Grad School. We were cordial, we tolerated each other and displayed the usual courtesies, but we both knew there was no love between us. That morning, he had an extra edge.

"Wayne, you are a very great guy. We like you a lot. Everyone does. But recently, you just seem to not be meeting our expectations as a leader," Vito stoically recanted. "We want to work with you; we tried. Your staff looks to you for your support, and frankly, you haven't been there for them. You haven't been for some time now. You're consistently late for meetings. We can't continue like this, Wayne. It's setting a bad precedent.

You've led our flagship site over the years, a great leader, and an invaluable contributor to the site. You've been a great ambassador for our organization locally and nationally. But unfortunately, we must ask for your resignation." Vito's words ate into me, and his words hung heavily in the air.

There was a buzz in my ears. My mouth felt dry. I became nauseous and felt my armpits sweating. A visual of all my years at the agency flashed backward like a cinematic film in my mind. I stood there numb and dumbfounded. I took a deep breath and felt a weirdness settle in the pit of my stomach. It took everything out of me to hold back the tears.

This was my SHIFT moment!

My message to the fellas: When the Shift hits the man, the man must make a Shift (Title of my upcoming book). Transformation takes place from the inside out. For my BS downward slope to change, my being "stuck in a rut" needing MORE needing to break free and becoming a victor rather than a midlife crisis victim, I knew there in that moment it was time to SHIFT my mindset to SHIFT my life.

Up until then, I refused to accept that my world was imploding; that I needed help. I had been fighting to hold on to my big old male-ego identity. I was still the man, if only in my head. This old Self no longer served me. I was hurting those that I cared for and loved most. Especially me.

A year after that revelation of my extramarital affair and the birth of my beautiful baby boy, Jared, my ex had moved on with her life, 'coming out" as a lesbian. I took the news very personally. My fragile ego was bruised more profoundly. Had I been that terrible a partner? A poor lover?

A year of therapy subsequently helped me to cope with my traumas and injured male ego, but not before I had fallen from my perch on top of the proverbial hill. I had lost approximately 30 lbs. since the year following my breakup. I affirmed during this recognizant and recovery period to never again cheat on any woman. Since I then had two impressionable daughters and two sons, it was time to model appropriate Manhood.

After the Shift, I committed to myself, and secretly, on behalf of Black men everywhere to be the best dad, the most loving, understanding, and present father ever. I made the same commitment as a leader to whomever I worked with in the future. I was determined that any person with whom I developed a personal or professional relationship would become a bigger, bolder, better version of themselves after THE SHIFT.

Despite a few episodes of life-threatening illnesses that hospitalized me in my 40s and 50s due to reckless abandonment of self-care, today I have the strength and energy of men 20 years my junior. I've added lean muscle mass, paid strict attention to my diet as a vegan, and exercise routine. Regarding my romantic life, in my relationships, with my children and family, my new wife, Audrey, had been friends, and we dated almost 3 decades ago at City College, New York.

I applied the law of attraction and manifestation, principles that I teach in my coaching, to bring her back into my life. We are fully committed and gleeful partners in our marriage, not simply striving but thriving. We share an amazing, blended family, including all the parents of our children and their current partners.

My transformation did not happen overnight. Some 20 years later, my transformative journey continues. I pivoted to a new career and leveled up my professional self, vacating the comfort of the not-for-profit world that

I had come to know so well and excelled in. I plunged headfirst into the uncertain waters of Corporate America.

When we SHIFT, we must assess risks and act despite the fear of failure, embarrassment, loss, or even death. I succeeded as a leader in corporate for eight years, leaving at my discretion. This time, I decided to fire my employers and dive head-first into entrepreneurship.

Here are the 3-stages of The SHIFT I learned and have successfully helped scores of black men to achieve in my signature VIP Transformative Coaching Program:

1. *Values and Beliefs SHIFT – During crisis or a "crash" period in your life, your core values must be explored and aligned with and drive your beliefs, thoughts, words, actions, habits and outcomes...your personal reality or identity. Our (old) beliefs must be evaluated and reframed to serve us and those around us.*

2. *Identity SHIFT – This is a huge one and takes time and energy. Your Ego often is your primary undoing. It keeps you in the proverbial "Man Box." Shift or transformation is only possible when you are willing to let go of the old you. Identity Shift happens when we start claiming and acting like the Man we wish to become. A (w)holistic man!*

3. *Purpose SHIFT – Our purpose is ordained. Knowing that you are unique and divinely designed to fulfill a mission that ONLY you are called to fulfill is both intimidating but also liberating. When you remove your limiting beliefs about what's possible, supported by your values, and adapt an identity of "YOU are capable" ... your purpose will reveal itself to you!*

Coaching and helping Black men (and the women who love them) how to prepare for, avoid, and overcome midlife transitions or crises is my birthright. I was born and compelled to fulfill this purpose. This is my deep soul calling that I had been stalling. By applying my signature VIP Transformational coaching strategies, I served scores of men (and the women who love them) to get beyond midlife hurdles, and to live lives feeling more significant, more certain and more complete.

Through my coaching, writing, and speaking, I am on a mission to raise awareness and provide tools and strategies for thousands of Black men who may exhibit learned hopelessness, helplessness, and worthlessness, to break free and discover a world of power, purpose, peace, prosperity, and endless possibilities in the Second Half of their lives.

And I will see you at the top!

Coach Wayne

http://viptransformativeliving.com

Boysen Hodgson

Slow Learner.

Men's work did not come easily to me. For years I thought I was different, special, above-it-all – that my intellect, a bookshelf full of self-help, and some mediocre meditation was going to score me in the top 5% at "Good Guy University."

In my early twenties, I committed to a relationship that proved just how deeply flawed my self-perception was.

Seven years later, many mornings before leaving for work, I would find myself standing at the window, trying to not panic. I would look out into the yard and try to just keep breathing. Coffee mug in one hand, cigarette in the other, I would take deep drags and focus as hard as I could to calm my pounding heart, to slow my bouncing legs, to release the vise from my chest.

Sunlight through the trees and a gentle breeze through the screen door, the overwhelming green of the woods and weeds, the condensation between reclaimed panes from sliding glass doors. All I felt was how afraid I was, how ashamed, how angry, how trapped.

About a year earlier, my Mom passed, on Friday September 13, 2002. I wasn't there when she died. The last time I had seen her, sitting next to the bed where she was quickly being devoured by cancer, I told her I was staying in the relationship. She smiled with such sadness, tears running down her face. In the year after her death, the reality of the suffering grew worse.

The world shrunk around me. I chose again and again to cut off relationships with friends and family, to retreat from responsibility, to hide from the life I had created. I was in a job with nowhere to go, in a relationship that brought extraordinary pain, and living without a single person to confide in.

Shame had me keeping secrets, and fear kept me living small.

I broke my daily cyclone of anxious thoughts with pleasure-seeking and numbing. When I was working, I poured all my attention into pleasing people. When I was out of work, I spent money I didn't have on fast-food, cigarettes, and stacks of movie rentals to fill the long hours of night.

The storms of the relationship came in crashing humiliating waves. I would go in cycles, secretly consuming porn, failing to take responsibility with money, lying to cover it all, doubling down on being 'better,' continuously smashing the crumbs of a too-fragile trust. I would rage in shame and helplessness, then consume her hatred and disgust as penance, spoiled food for my self-loathing.

I believed I deserved the repulsion I frequently experienced.

I always knew there were other possibilities. I had seen and been told about the ManKind Project and its New Warrior weekend and men's groups by my brothers, some of whom had been participating for years. I had heard about integrity. I had witnessed emotional connection. I longed for the brotherhood I witnessed there, but could never touch it.

I even tried a couple times to connect with a local men's organization, but quickly retreated when I realized I might begin telling the truth about my choices. That felt impossible.

With my growing levels of anxiety, eventually I sought individual therapy.

In therapy the belief that I deserved disgust, and that I had to hide in order to be loved, began to unravel. I started learning to tell the truth and face difficult consequences. I started learning how to say what I felt. This hastened a final end to the relationship. I was not graceful. Mostly I was full of resentment and blame.

But in the aftermath, I began to take some responsibility for my healing. Within a month, I quit smoking, started riding my bike and getting work done on my body. I reconnected with my family, and began the slow process of repairing relationships.

Less than a year later I met the woman who would become my wife.

And this is when my men's work journey truly began. I began my new relationship with an embarrassing, painful, and drawn out disclosure of all the dark reasons I believed myself to be unlovable. I didn't want to hide anymore. She was definitely knocked on her heels, but she didn't run.

I found in her a beautiful, sharp, kind, and powerful woman with a clear understanding of who she is and what she is worth. We connected easily and deeply and found joy in working and playing together. And yet, six months in, I was subtly recreating the patterns of secrecy, shame, and fear that had doomed every other relationship. She sensed it. She called it out. And on a bridge we built together over a stream we had crossed together nearly every day we had shared, I got honest again.

I didn't want to lose the remarkable love that was growing within me. I was terrified to do something different, but I knew it was time.

Part of my healing practice was seeing a chiropractor. After one particularly popping adjustment, I stayed lying face down on the table with tears streaming down my face. When I had pulled myself together and made my way into the hallway, the chiropractor, Wayne, followed me out. He told me he could see I was 'going through it,' and he asked if I had ever heard of the New Warrior Training. I laughed, and I swore at him.

Within a couple weeks, after talking with my partner, I signed up.

The weekend came. I was surrounded by men in a cauldron for men's expression. I was terrified. I saw other men share what was tearing them apart, collapsing in sobs of relief. I hung back as long as I could. But when I stepped out for my time, the secrets I had kept and the shame I had nurtured my whole life came howling from every pore. I felt the rage I repressed watching my father shamelessly hurt one woman after another for years, including my Mom. I felt the resentment toward my mother for her loving but deeply shaming efforts to raise 'good boys.' And most of all, I finally faced the gauntlet of denial I had built to protect myself that was robbing me of the thing I wanted most, a loving and truthful relationship.

That was 20 years ago. Today, I am married to that fierce woman who called me forward. Today, I am committed to doing the work it takes to stay in a loving and truthful partnership. It's simple, but it's not easy. After all, I'm a slow learner. For me, that means I continue my men's work. I continue to meet with men willing to see me, love and support me, and challenge me – in all my pain and all my beauty.

Whatever you may be hiding from, this is available to you.

Boysen Hodgson
http://boysenh.com

Always remember, transformation is an ongoing process. Commit to the process and learn to trust it, and it will guide you to exactly the right place you need to go.

The rainbow is a part of nature, and you have to be in the right place to see it. It's beautiful, all of the colors, even the colors you can't see. That really fit us as a people because we are all of the colors. Our sexuality is all of the colors. We are all the genders, races, and ages.
— Gilbert Baker

CHAPTER 5

A New Conversation About Sex

Understanding the Impact of "Sex Sells" Culture

In today's society, the pervasive and influential "sex sells" culture has deeply ingrained itself into our collective consciousness, shaping not only our perceptions of sexuality and relationships but also influencing our sense of self-worth and identity. This culture leverages the power of sexual imagery and messages to captivate attention, evoke desire, and drive consumer behavior across a wide spectrum of industries.

From the glossy pages of magazines to the screens of our devices, from the billboards lining city streets to the lyrics of popular songs, we are inundated with depictions of hyper-sexualized bodies, explicit content, and the glamorization of promiscuous behavior. The constant bombardment of these sexualized messages can imprint upon our psyches and contribute to a distorted view of what is considered attractive, desirable, and socially acceptable in terms of sexual expression and relationships.

The roots of the "sex sells" culture can be traced back to the early days of advertising and marketing, where the association between sex and commercial success became firmly established. Marketers capitalize on the primal human instinct for reproduction and desire, tapping into deep-seated emotions and instincts to create a powerful connection between their products and sexual appeal. This strategy has proven effective in capturing consumer attention, generating buzz, and driving sales, leading to the perpetuation of sexualized content across various media platforms.

Beyond the surface allure of sex appeal and titillation, the "sex sells" culture operates on a deeper level, permeating societal norms, perpetuating harmful stereotypes, and reinforcing entrenched power dynamics. This culture often equates worth with physical appearance, perpetuates gender-based discrimination, and commodifies human intimacy and connection. By promoting unrealistic beauty standards and narrow definitions of masculinity and femininity, it can sow seeds of self-doubt, insecurity, and alienation among individuals who do not fit the idealized mold.

Moreover, the "sex sells" culture not only impacts individuals on a personal level but also contributes to broader societal issues such as toxic masculinity, objectification, and the normalization of unhealthy relationship dynamics. It can foster a culture where consent is blurred, boundaries are crossed, and intimacy becomes synonymous with exploitation rather than genuine connection.

In this context, cultivating critical thinking skills and media literacy becomes essential to navigate the complexities of the "sex sells" culture and its implications on our lives. By actively engaging with and questioning the messages and imagery presented to us, we can begin to discern between empowering representations of sexuality and harmful stereotypes perpetuated for profit. By choosing to consume content that aligns with our values of respect, authenticity, and inclusivity, we can actively challenge the narratives that perpetuate harmful attitudes towards sex and relationships.

Ultimately, dismantling the pervasive influence of the "sex sells" culture requires a collective effort to reshape societal attitudes, challenge harmful norms, and advocate for a more compassionate and equitable representation of human sexuality and intimacy. By acknowledging the power dynamics at play in media and advertising, we can take steps towards reclaiming agency over our own beliefs, desires, and relationships, fostering a culture that values genuine connection, mutual respect, and holistic well-being.

Redefining Success for Men Beyond Sexual Conquests

In a society that often equates a man's worth with his ability to attract and conquer sexual partners, it is vital to challenge this narrow definition of success. True success for men transcends the shallow metrics of conquests and embraces a more holistic approach to self-fulfillment.

Men are often socialized to equate their masculinity with the number of sexual partners they have had, perpetuating a toxic cycle of validation through external measures. However, this limited perspective neglects the richness of human experience beyond physical intimacy.

Real success for men encompasses a multifaceted journey of self-discovery, personal growth, and emotional intelligence. It involves cultivating deep and meaningful connections with others, nurturing empathy and compassion, and contributing positively to one's community and the world at large.

By redefining success in terms of inner fulfillment and genuine human connections, men can break free from the constraints of societal expectations and forge their own paths based on authenticity and integrity. Instead of measuring themselves by external markers of conquest, they can seek fulfillment in embodying qualities such as vulnerability, empathy, and kindness.

This shift in perspective not only benefits men individually but also has the power to transform societal norms around masculinity and relationships. Men who prioritize emotional well-being and genuine connections create a ripple effect of positivity, inspiring others to embrace a more holistic and compassionate view of success.

Ultimately, true success for men lies in their ability to navigate the complexities of modern life with grace, authenticity, and a deep sense of connection to themselves and others. It is a journey of self-discovery and growth that transcends societal expectations and embraces the profound beauty of human connection and emotional intelligence.

On this journey towards authentic success, men may encounter challenges and setbacks, but it is through these experiences that they can cultivate resilience, self-awareness, and a deeper understanding of themselves. Embracing vulnerability and facing adversity with courage and resilience are crucial aspects of personal growth and development.

Additionally, men can find fulfillment in cultivating a sense of purpose beyond their individual desires, whether through serving their communities, championing social causes, or engaging in creative pursuits that uplift and inspire others. By contributing positively to the world around them, men can find a deeper sense of fulfillment and purpose that transcends fleeting measures of success.

In essence, true success for men is a journey of self-discovery, growth, and contribution that goes beyond societal expectations and shallow validations. By seeking authentic connections, embodying empathy and kindness, and pursuing a path of purpose and integrity, men can redefine success on their own terms and lead lives of meaning and authenticity.

Challenging Cultural Norms about Men and Sex

In this section, we delve into the deeply ingrained cultural norms and stereotypes that often shape men's views and experiences of sex. From a young age, many boys are conditioned to believe that their worth is tied to their sexual prowess and conquests. Society often celebrates men who have multiple sexual partners, equating it with masculinity and success. This pressure to conform to certain ideals of manhood can have damaging effects on men's mental health and relationships.

Men are frequently taught to suppress their emotions and vulnerability in the context of sex, perpetuating a disconnect between their physical experiences and emotional needs. This can lead to feelings of emptiness and dissatisfaction despite engaging in sexual activities that society deems desirable. The emphasis on performance and dominance in sexual encounters can overshadow the importance of genuine connection, mutual respect, and consent.

To challenge these harmful cultural norms, men must embark on a journey of self-discovery and introspection. They need to unlearn limiting beliefs about their sexuality and redefine their relationship with sex on their terms. This process requires courage, vulnerability, and a willingness to confront societal expectations head-on. By embracing a more holistic and inclusive approach to sex, men can cultivate healthier attitudes towards intimacy, pleasure, and self-expression.

Moreover, men must also confront the toxic masculinity that often permeates discussions around sex and relationships. By deconstructing harmful stereotypes and promoting positive representations of masculinity, men can create a more supportive and understanding environment for themselves and others. Embracing diversity, inclusivity, and empathy in conversations about sex can empower men to explore their desires, boundaries, and identities without judgment or shame.

In essence, challenging cultural norms about men and sex involves dismantling the rigid constructs that limit male expression and perpetuate harmful gender roles. By fostering a culture of authenticity, communication, and respect, men can embark on a journey towards a more fulfilling and satisfying relationship with themselves and their partners. It is through introspection, awareness, and a willingness to break free from societal constraints that men can truly embrace their sexual identities with confidence and autonomy.

This journey of self-discovery may also lead to a deeper understanding of the intersectionality of gender, sexuality, and power dynamics. Men can begin to acknowledge the privilege and responsibility that come with their social position while striving to be allies in the quest for gender equality and sexual liberation. By engaging in conversations about consent, boundaries, and respect, men can help create a safer and more inclusive sexual culture for all individuals.

Furthermore, men can benefit from exploring the concept of sexual ethics – understanding the importance of honesty, communication, and consent in all intimate interactions. By prioritizing the well-being and pleasure of themselves and their partners, men can foster more meaningful and fulfilling connections that transcend societal expectations and stereotypes. This shift towards a more conscious and compassionate approach to sex can lead to greater intimacy, satisfaction, and personal growth for men seeking to redefine their relationship with their own desires and identities.

Authenticity in Sexual Expression

In a world where societal expectations and norms often dictate how we should express our sexuality, it can be challenging to find the courage to be truly authentic. Authenticity in sexual expression goes beyond simply being honest about your desires and boundaries; it is a profound exploration of your innermost self, your truest desires, and your deepest fears.

Being authentic in your sexual expression means delving into the core of your being and embracing all aspects of your sexuality without judgment or shame. It's about understanding your own needs and wants, honoring your boundaries, and communicating openly and honestly with your partner. Authenticity requires self-awareness, self-acceptance, and the willingness to confront and challenge societal constructs that may have inhibited your true self from fully emerging.

When you embody authenticity in your sexual expression, you create a sacred space where vulnerability and intimacy can thrive. This vulnerability allows for deep connection and emotional resonance with your partner, fostering a sense of trust and mutual understanding that can transcend physical intimacy.

Moreover, authenticity in sexual expression involves being attuned to the present moment and fully engaging with your partner in a mindful and conscious way. It means letting go of pretenses and allowing yourself to be seen and understood for who you truly are. This level of authenticity cultivates a sense of liberation and empowerment, as you embrace your sexuality with confidence and self-assurance.

Embracing authenticity in sexual expression is a journey of self-discovery and personal growth. It requires ongoing reflection, introspection, and a commitment to continually explore and honor your evolving desires and boundaries. By being true to yourself and allowing your authentic self to shine through in your sexual expression, you open yourself up to a world of profound intimacy, connection, and fulfillment.

This journey towards authenticity may involve unlearning societal conditioning, confronting internalized shame or guilt, and embracing vulnerability as a strength rather than a weakness. It requires a willingness to be honest with yourself and your partner, even when the truth may be difficult or uncomfortable. Authentic sexual expression also involves respecting the boundaries and desires of your partner, engaging in open and honest communication, and fostering a sense of mutual trust and respect.

As you continue on this journey towards authentic sexual expression, you may find that it opens up new pathways for self-discovery, growth, and connection. It can lead to a deeper understanding of yourself and your partner, as well as a greater appreciation for the beauty and complexity of human sexuality. By embracing authenticity in your sexual expression, you not only honor your own truth but also create space for deep intimacy, connection, and fulfillment to flourish in your relationships.

The Courage of Celibacy and Emotional Intimacy

In a society that often glorifies and prioritizes sexual conquests and experiences, the idea of celibacy can be seen as unconventional and even challenging. However, the decision to embrace celibacy is a courageous one that can lead to profound emotional growth and intimacy.

Celibacy is not just about abstaining from physical intimacy; it is a deliberate choice to focus on developing emotional connections and building deeper relationships. By redirecting our energy and attention away from fleeting physical pleasures, we open ourselves up to a deeper level of emotional intimacy with others.

Choosing celibacy requires a high level of self-awareness and self-control. It allows individuals to reflect on their desires, motivations, and values, leading to a greater understanding of themselves and their needs. By practicing celibacy, individuals can cultivate a sense of inner peace and fulfillment that comes from aligning their actions with their higher values and beliefs.

Emotional intimacy, on the other hand, is about forming authentic connections with others based on trust, vulnerability, and genuine communication. It involves sharing our thoughts, feelings, and experiences in a way that fosters understanding and closeness. Emotional intimacy enriches our relationships and allows us to feel truly seen and supported by those around us.

Combining celibacy with a focus on emotional intimacy can be a powerful way to deepen our connections with others. By choosing to prioritize emotional intimacy over physical gratification, we create the space for genuine and meaningful relationships to flourish. This requires courage, vulnerability, and a willingness to be open and honest with ourselves and our partners.

Embracing celibacy and emotional intimacy is not without its challenges, but the rewards can be profound. By stepping away from societal expectations and embracing a path of emotional connection and self-discovery, individuals can experience a heightened sense of fulfillment, authenticity, and growth in their relationships with others. Ultimately, the courage to pursue celibacy and emotional intimacy can lead to deeper connections, greater self-awareness, and a richer, more meaningful life.

Celibacy and emotional intimacy go hand in hand, creating a strong foundation for personal growth and meaningful connections. By respecting our own boundaries and honoring our need for emotional closeness, we cultivate relationships built on trust, respect, and genuine connection. This journey towards celibacy and emotional intimacy requires patience, self-reflection, and a willingness to explore the depths of our emotions and desires.

As we navigate the complexities of our inner worlds and the dynamics of our relationships, celibacy can serve as a powerful tool for self-discovery and personal empowerment. It allows us to prioritize our emotional well-being and foster connections based on mutual understanding and respect. By embracing celibacy and emotional intimacy, we embark on a journey of self-discovery and genuine connection that can enrich our lives and relationships in ways we may never have imagined.

In a world that often measures success and fulfillment by external standards, choosing celibacy and focusing on emotional intimacy can be a radical act of self-love and empowerment. It challenges us to redefine our understanding of intimacy and connection, prioritizing emotional depth and authenticity over superficial gratification. Through this intentional practice, we can cultivate relationships that nourish our souls and bring a sense of purpose and meaning to our lives.

Breaking Free from Sex Addiction and Pornography

Breaking Free from Sex Addiction and Pornography:

Sex addiction and pornography addiction are complex and insidious issues that can have profound impacts on individuals' mental, emotional, and physical well-being. The pervasive accessibility of sexual content and explicit material in today's digital age has only exacerbated these addictive behaviors, leading many individuals down a path of compulsive and destructive patterns.

Recognizing the signs of sex addiction and pornography addiction is crucial in confronting and addressing these issues. Common signs may include chronic preoccupation with sexual thoughts and activities, engaging in risky sexual behaviors, experiencing distress or guilt after sexual encounters, and a persistent inability to control or limit one's sexual behaviors. It is essential to distinguish between healthy sexual expression and addictive behaviors that negatively impact one's life and relationships.

Understanding the root causes of sex addiction and pornography addiction is essential in formulating an effective treatment plan. For some individuals, addiction may be linked to unresolved trauma, childhood experiences, or underlying mental health disorders. Exploring these underlying factors with the support of a therapist or counselor can help individuals uncover the emotional wounds driving their addictive behaviors and work towards healing and recovery.

Seeking professional help is a critical step in breaking free from sex addiction and pornography addiction. Therapy provides a safe and confidential space to explore the underlying issues contributing to addiction, learn healthy coping strategies, and develop tools for managing triggers and cravings. Cognitive-behavioral therapy (CBT), group therapy, and other evidence-based treatments can be highly effective in supporting individuals on their journey to recovery.

Building a supportive network of peers, friends, or family members can also play a vital role in the recovery process. Connecting with others who understand and empathize with the challenges of addiction can provide a sense of community and encouragement. Support groups, such as Sex Addicts Anonymous or Pornography Anonymous, offer a platform for individuals to share their experiences, receive guidance, and find solidarity in their recovery efforts.

Self-care practices, such as mindfulness, exercise, and healthy lifestyle choices, are essential in maintaining emotional and physical well-being during the recovery process. Engaging in activities that bring joy, relaxation, and fulfillment can help individuals create a sense of balance and purpose outside of addictive behaviors. Developing self-compassion and acceptance is also crucial in overcoming feelings of shame and self-judgment that often accompany addiction.

Recovery from sex addiction and pornography addiction is a challenging and ongoing journey that requires dedication, commitment, and perseverance. It is essential for individuals to be patient with themselves, celebrate small victories, and seek help when needed. By confronting their addiction, seeking support, and making positive changes in their lives, individuals can break free from the grip of sex addiction and pornography addiction and embrace a healthier, more fulfilling way of living.

Recovery from addiction is not a linear process; individuals may experience setbacks and relapses along the way. Recognizing these challenges as part of the journey and learning from them can be crucial in moving forward and strengthening one's commitment to recovery. It is important for individuals to practice self-compassion and avoid self-criticism when facing setbacks, as this can hinder progress.

In some cases, medication may be prescribed to help manage underlying mental health conditions that contribute to sex addiction or pornography addiction. It is essential for individuals to work closely with a healthcare provider to determine the most appropriate treatment plan for their unique needs. Medication, when used in conjunction with therapy and other interventions, can support individuals in managing symptoms and achieving long-term recovery.

As individuals progress in their recovery journey, it is important for them to establish healthy boundaries and routines to maintain their progress. Setting boundaries around technology and limiting exposure to triggers, such as explicit content or risky environments, can help individuals avoid relapse and stay on track with their recovery goals. Establishing a daily routine that prioritizes self-care, mindfulness, and healthy habits can also support individuals in staying connected to their recovery journey.

Rebuilding relationships that may have been strained or damaged due to sex addiction or pornography addiction is an essential aspect of recovery. Open and honest communication with loved ones, seeking forgiveness when necessary, and actively working to repair trust can help individuals heal the relational wounds caused by addiction. Engaging in couples therapy or family therapy can provide a supportive environment for repairing and strengthening relationships affected by addiction.

Ultimately, breaking free from sex addiction and pornography addiction requires courage, vulnerability, and a willingness to confront difficult emotions and experiences. By seeking help, building a support network, engaging in therapy, and practicing self-compassion, individuals can embark on a path toward healing, growth, and a life free from the grip of addiction. Embracing a future filled with healthy relationships, personal fulfillment, and emotional well-being is within reach for those who choose to take the first steps toward recovery.

Cultivating Body Positivity and Sexual Confidence

In a world where standards of beauty and sexuality are often unrealistic and unattainable, cultivating body positivity and sexual confidence is crucial for maintaining mental and emotional well-being. Embracing one's own body, regardless of shape, size, or imperfections, is a radical act of self-love and empowerment.

Body positivity is a philosophy that encourages individuals to accept and celebrate their bodies just as they are. It involves recognizing that beauty comes in all shapes, sizes, and forms, challenging societal norms that dictate a narrow definition of attractiveness. By embracing our bodies with love and acceptance, we can reclaim our sense of self-worth and break free from the toxic messages that tell us we are not good enough.

Practicing body positivity also involves self-care rituals that prioritize our physical and mental well-being. This can include nourishing our bodies with nutritious foods, engaging in joyful movement that feels good to us, getting enough rest, and engaging in practices that promote mental wellness, such as mindfulness and self-compassion.

Moreover, body positivity goes beyond just individual acceptance. It also calls for societal change to dismantle harmful beauty standards and promote inclusivity and diversity in media and popular culture. By advocating for representation of all body types in mainstream platforms, we can create a more inclusive and accepting society where everyone feels valued and celebrated for who they are.

On the other hand, sexual confidence is about feeling comfortable and empowered in expressing our desires and boundaries in intimate relationships. It involves owning our sexuality and asserting our needs without shame or guilt. Communication is a key aspect of sexual confidence, as being able to express our wants and needs to our partners creates a space for mutual respect and understanding.

Building body positivity and sexual confidence is a journey that requires patience and self-reflection. It involves challenging ingrained beliefs about beauty and sexuality, embracing our bodies with kindness and compassion, and surrounding ourselves with people who uplift and support us in our journey of self-acceptance.

Ultimately, cultivating body positivity and sexual confidence is a radical act of self-love that can have a profound impact on our overall well-being and relationships. By embracing ourselves fully and authentically, we can live more fulfilling and joyous lives.

The only way to do great work is to love what you do. If you haven't found it yet, keep looking. Don't settle.
— Steve Jobs

CHAPTER 6

Vocational Arousal – Finding Your Passion

The Pursuit of Passion

In a world where the noise of everyday life can drown out the whispers of our true desires, the pursuit of passion becomes a sacred mission, a quest for self-discovery and fulfillment that goes beyond the superficial trappings of success and status. It is a calling, a primal force that resonates deep within our being, urging us to break free from the chains of conformity and embrace the unique essence of who we are meant to be.

Passion is not merely a fleeting interest or a passing phase; it is a flame that burns eternal, lighting the path to our dreams and illuminating the darkest corners of our souls. It is the source of our greatest joys and our deepest sorrows, the wellspring of creativity, innovation, and resilience that empowers us to overcome any obstacle in our path.

Yet, the pursuit of passion is not without its challenges. It requires courage to listen to the whispers of our hearts amidst the clamor of societal expectations and norms. It demands vulnerability to embrace our true selves unapologetically, even in the face of criticism or rejection.

It necessitates perseverance to weather the storms of doubt, uncertainty, and fear that may arise along the way.

But within these challenges lies the opportunity for growth, transformation, and self-actualization. As we delve into the depths of our passions, we unearth hidden talents, unlock untapped potential, and forge connections that bridge the gap between who we are and who we aspire to become. We learn to trust in the wisdom of our intuition, to honor the guidance of our inner voice, and to surrender to the unfolding of our unique destiny with grace and humility.

The pursuit of passion is a journey of self-discovery, a quest for authenticity and alignment that leads us to the heart of our true purpose and the core of our deepest desires. It is a testament to the infinite potential that resides within each of us, a reminder that we are bound only by the limits of our imagination and the constraints of our own making.

So let us embrace the pursuit of passion with open hearts and open minds, knowing that in its pursuit, we will not only discover the essence of who we are but also unleash the untapped potential that lies dormant within us, waiting to be awakened and unleashed upon the world. For in the pursuit of passion, we find not only fulfillment but also the key to unlocking our true power and living a life of profound purpose and meaning.

Rethinking Success and Fulfillment

In a world where the clamor for external validation often drowns out the whispers of our inner selves, it can be challenging to redefine our understanding of success and fulfillment. We are bombarded with societal standards that equate success with material wealth, fame, and power, leading many to believe that happiness lies in the accumulation of these external markers. However, true fulfillment cannot be bought or borrowed; it must be cultivated from within.

Rethinking success requires a shift in perspective, a conscious choice to peel back the layers of societal conditioning and listen to the quiet voice of our authentic selves. It demands introspection, self-awareness, and a willingness to embrace vulnerability, uncertainty, and discomfort. Success, when redefined through the lens of fulfillment, becomes a journey of self-discovery, self-acceptance, and self-expression.

To find true fulfillment, we must align our actions with our values, passions, and purpose. It is about living a life that is in harmony with our core beliefs, honoring our unique strengths and talents, and contributing to the greater good. Success, in this redefined sense, is not a destination to reach but a way of being—a continuous process of growth, learning, and evolution.

When we let go of external validations and embrace our intrinsic worth, we open ourselves up to a deeper sense of fulfillment that transcends fleeting achievements and accolades. It is a state of being anchored in gratitude, compassion, and connection—with ourselves, with others, and with the world at large. By redefining success through the lens of fulfillment, we not only enrich our own lives but also inspire those around us to do the same.

True fulfillment is about finding joy in the journey rather than fixating on the destination. It is about savoring the moments of connection, the small victories, and the personal growth that come from stepping outside our comfort zones. When we shift our focus from external measures of success to internal markers of fulfillment, we liberate ourselves from the constraints of societal expectations and carve our paths based on our innate desires and values.

By embracing a mindset of abundance rather than scarcity, we cultivate a sense of gratitude for the present moment and trust in the unfolding of our unique paths. Fulfillment is not a one-size-fits-all concept—it is deeply personal and subjective, rooted in our individual experiences, dreams, and aspirations. When we honor our true selves and align our actions with our inner truths, we tap into a wellspring of fulfillment that sustains us through life's ups and downs.

In the pursuit of fulfillment, we are invited to explore the depths of our souls, confront our fears and insecurities, and embrace our vulnerabilities with courage and compassion. It is a journey that requires us to confront the shadows within us, to confront the shadows within us, to confront the shadows within us, to confront the shadows within us, to confront the shadows within us, to confront the shadows within us, to confront the shadows within us, to confront the shadows within us, to confront the shadows within us, to confront the shadows within us, to confront the shadows within us, to confront the shadows within usd embrace the light that shines from our core being.

When we redefine success through the lens of fulfillment, we transcend the limitations of ego-driven ambitions and tap into a wellspring of purpose and meaning. It is a shift in consciousness, a reimagining of our priorities and values, that allows us to craft a life that is in alignment with our deepest truths and highest aspirations. Success is no longer measured by external accolades but by the depth of our connections, the authenticity of our actions, and the impact we make in the lives of others.

In the tapestry of life, fulfillment weaves a thread of resilience, compassion, and authenticity that binds us together in a shared journey of growth and transformation. As we embrace the richness of our inner worlds and cultivate a sense of wholeness and harmony within ourselves, we pave the way for a more compassionate, connected, and fulfilling existence for all beings on this beautiful planet we call home.

Unveiling Your Inner Calling

In this section, we will delve into the process of unveiling your inner calling. Discovering your true purpose and passion in life is a journey that often requires deep introspection, self-awareness, and courage. It involves exploring your values, interests, strengths, and dreams to uncover what truly ignites your soul.

Many individuals go through life feeling a sense of emptiness or dissatisfaction because they are not aligned with their inner calling. They may be pursuing a career or lifestyle that society deems successful or prestigious, yet deep down, they feel a lack of fulfillment.

Unveiling your inner calling requires you to quiet the noise of external expectations and listen to the whispers of your heart. It involves reconnecting with your intuition and inner wisdom to uncover what truly resonates with your essence.

Through introspective practices such as journaling, meditation, and mindfulness, you can begin to peel back the layers of conditioning and societal pressures to reveal your authentic self and deepest desires.

As you embark on this journey of self-discovery, remember that your inner calling may evolve and change over time. It is a process of constant growth and self-awareness, requiring openness to new possibilities and the courage to follow your heart.

By unveiling your inner calling, you can align your life with your true purpose and passion, leading to a sense of fulfillment, meaning, and joy in all that you do.

To truly uncover your inner calling, it is essential to examine your past experiences, both positive and negative, for the valuable lessons they hold. Reflect on moments when you felt most alive, fulfilled, and in alignment with your true self. These instances can offer clues as to what truly resonates with your soul and can guide you towards your purpose.

Additionally, engaging in activities that bring you joy and a sense of flow can provide further insight into your inner calling. Pay attention to the activities that make you lose track of time and fill you with a deep sense of satisfaction; these are often indicators of where your true passion lies.

In your quest to unveil your inner calling, it is crucial to be patient and compassionate with yourself. This process of self-discovery takes time and requires vulnerability and openness to exploring different facets of your being. Embrace the journey with an open heart and a willingness to embrace the unknown.

Remember that your inner calling is unique to you and may not necessarily align with societal expectations or norms. Trust in your intuition and inner guidance to lead you towards the path that is meant for you, even if it diverges from the conventional route.

Through the unveiling of your inner calling, you have the opportunity to live a life of authenticity, purpose, and fulfillment. Embrace the journey with courage and curiosity, and allow your true essence to shine brightly in all that you do.

Breaking Free from Societal Expectations

In breaking free from the constraints of societal expectations, we embark on a profound journey of self-discovery and self-empowerment. This journey is not merely a whimsical escape from the burdens of conformity but a deliberate and intentional act of reclaiming our true essence, our authentic identity that may have been obscured by the demands of the external world. It is a process of excavation, of digging deep into the layers of our being to uncover the raw, unfiltered truth that lies at our core.

As we navigate the twists and turns of this inner odyssey, we are confronted with the shadows of our past, the echoes of conditioning that have shaped our beliefs and influenced our choices. We are forced to confront our deepest fears, our insecurities, and the self-imposed limitations that have held us captive in a state of mediocrity. It is in this crucible of self-examination that we find the opportunity for transformation, for growth, and for the blossoming of our true potential.

Breaking free requires courage – a courage that is not brash or reckless but rooted in a profound sense of self-awareness and self-compassion. It is a willingness to confront the parts of ourselves that we may have kept hidden, the vulnerabilities that make us human, and the wounds that have yet to heal. It is a commitment to embracing our imperfections, our flaws, and our idiosyncrasies with a sense of grace and acceptance, recognizing that these qualities are what make us unique, what make us whole.

In the act of breaking free, we are not just liberating ourselves from the shackles of societal expectations; we are also forging a new path forward, a path that is guided by our inner truth, our deepest values, and our most authentic desires. We are stepping into the fullness of who we are – unapologetically, unabashedly, and unreservedly – and in doing so, we are setting a powerful example for others to follow.

It is in the breaking free that we find liberation, empowerment, and a renewed sense of purpose. It is a declaration of our sovereignty, a celebration of our individuality, and a testament to the resilience of the human spirit. And as we continue to walk this path of authenticity and self-discovery, may we remember that the true measure of our worth lies not in how well we conform to external standards but in how fully we embrace and express the unique essence of our being.

Embracing Vulnerability and Authenticity

In the delicate dance between vulnerability and authenticity, we find ourselves navigating the complex interplay of our innermost truths and outer expressions. To truly understand the power and depth of vulnerability, we must acknowledge its roots in the human experience - a shared journey of triumphs and tribulations, joys and sorrows, love and loss. In embracing our vulnerabilities, we unlock a gateway to profound self-discovery and growth, transcending the limitations of fear and shame that often shroud our authentic selves.

Authenticity, too, is a multifaceted gem that reflects the essence of our being in its purest form. It beckons us to delve deep into the reservoirs of our soul, to unearth the treasures of our unique perspective and intrinsic worth. When we commit to living authentically, we honor the intricate tapestry of our experiences, beliefs, and emotions, weaving a narrative that is rich in texture and resonance with our core values and aspirations.

The journey towards vulnerability and authenticity is not for the faint of heart. It requires a willingness to confront our innermost fears, to peel back the layers of societal conditioning and external expectations, and to stand boldly in the truth of who we are. It is a path of self-discovery and self-acceptance, a pilgrimage of the soul that demands courage, resilience, and unwavering faith in our own worthiness.

In the realm of creativity, vulnerability and authenticity serve as the alchemic catalysts that transform raw emotions into poignant art, bold ideas into groundbreaking innovation, and personal vulnerabilities into universal truths. When we allow ourselves to be seen and heard in our most authentic, vulnerable state, we invite others to witness the raw beauty of our humanity and connect on a deeper, more profound level.

It is through the lens of vulnerability and authenticity that we recognize the interconnectedness of our human experience, the universality of our struggles and triumphs, and the transformative power of genuine connection. In embracing our vulnerabilities and honoring our authenticity, we not only elevate our creative endeavors but also cultivate a deep sense of empathy, compassion, and understanding for ourselves and others.

As we journey deeper into the realm of vulnerability and authenticity, we uncover layers of wisdom, resilience, and grace that have been waiting to be unearthed within us. We learn to embrace the full spectrum of our emotions, to dance with the shadows and bask in the light, and to stand unapologetically in our own truth, no matter the storms that may rage around us.

Ultimately, it is in the embrace of vulnerability and the honoring of authenticity that we find the true essence of our humanity, forging connections that transcend time and space, and weaving a tapestry of authenticity and vulnerability that speaks to the hearts of all who dare to listen.

Cultivating a Mindset of Purpose

In order to truly cultivate a mindset of purpose, it is essential to first connect with your innermost self on a profound level. Dive into the depths of your being, exploring the intricate layers of your thoughts, emotions, and experiences to unveil the essence of who you are and what drives you. This introspective journey allows you to unearth the core values, beliefs, and passions that shape your identity and give meaning to your existence.

As you embark on this quest for self-discovery, it is crucial to approach it with openness, curiosity, and a willingness to confront any fears, doubts, or insecurities that may arise. Embracing vulnerability and authenticity in this process can lead to profound insights and revelations that illuminate your path towards purpose.

Understanding your purpose is not merely a cognitive exercise but a deeply personal and spiritual exploration that invites you to question societal norms, challenge limiting beliefs, and embrace your unique calling in the world. It requires a conscious effort to peel back the layers of conditioning and cultural expectations to reveal the pure essence of your soul and the innate gifts that lie within.

Once you have identified your purpose, the next step is to embody it fully in your everyday life. This involves aligning your thoughts, words, and actions with your guiding principles and staying true to your authentic self, even in the face of adversity or uncertainty. By living in alignment with your purpose, you cultivate a sense of integrity, authenticity, and inner harmony that infuses every aspect of your being.

Setting meaningful goals and intentions that align with your purpose is key to realizing your deepest desires and aspirations. By clarifying your vision for the future and taking intentional steps towards its manifestation, you create a sense of direction and focus that propels you forward on your journey towards purpose.

As you navigate the complexities of life, it is important to remain open to growth and evolution. Embrace the challenges and setbacks as opportunities for learning and transformation, allowing them to deepen your understanding of yourself and your purpose. Remember that your sense of purpose is dynamic and ever-evolving, expanding as you expand and resonating with the rhythm of your soul's journey.

Cultivating a mindset of purpose is not a solitary pursuit but a collaborative effort that involves seeking support and guidance from others who share your values and vision. Surround yourself with a community of like-minded individuals who uplift and inspire you, providing a sense of connection, belonging, and encouragement along your path towards purpose.

In conclusion, cultivating a mindset of purpose is an ongoing journey of self-discovery, growth, and self-expression that requires courage, commitment, and a deep willingness to listen to the whispers of your soul. By embracing your truest self, aligning your actions with your values, and staying open to the transformative power of purpose, you can create a life of depth, meaning, and fulfillment that resonates with the essence of who you are at your core.

Finding Balance and Well-being in Your Vocation

In the riveting tapestry of our professional pursuits and creative endeavors, there exists a profound imperative to navigate the labyrinthine pathways of our vocations with a steadfast commitment to nurturing our inner equilibrium and safeguarding our holistic well-being. Within the kaleidoscope of demands and expectations that define the landscape of our chosen vocations, we are called upon to meticulously tend to the delicate interplay between our professional pursuits and the intricate tapestry of our physical, emotional, and mental health.

Finding equilibrium in the whirlwind of our vocations necessitates a nuanced approach that honors the symbiotic relationship between our creative expressions and our overall well-being. Delving deep into the recesses of our soul, we unearth a myriad of emotions, experiences, and aspirations that inform the tapestry of our creative endeavors. It is within the fertile soil of our inner landscape that seeds of inspiration blossom into captivating narratives and dazzling artistic expressions that resonate with the collective heartbeat of humanity.

As we traverse the terrain of our vocations, it becomes paramount to cultivate a sense of balance that transcends the confines of mere productivity and performance metrics. By honoring the sacred dance between effort and rest, creation and contemplation, we carve out sacred spaces within our daily routines where our creativity can flourish amidst the clamor of external expectations. Embracing periods of stillness and introspection, we forge a deeper connection with our creative muses and tap into the wellspring of inspiration that flows ceaselessly through the corridors of our imagination.

Safeguarding our physical health amid the tumult of our vocations requires a steadfast commitment to honoring the temple of our body as a sacred vessel that carries us through the myriad chapters of our professional journey. Nourishing our bodies with wholesome foods, engaging in invigorating exercise routines, and embracing restorative practices that replenish our energy reserves serve as foundational pillars upon which we build a sustainable framework for enduring success and vitality.

Moreover, tending to our emotional and mental well-being within the framework of our vocations involves a profound commitment to cultivating self-awareness, emotional resilience, and compassion towards oneself and others. By nurturing a sense of mindfulness in our daily interactions, we begin to unravel the intricate layers of our inner landscape, peeling back the veil of distraction to reveal the raw authenticity that lies at the core of our being. Through practices of self-compassion, gratitude, and emotional regulation, we forge an unshakable foundation that empowers us to navigate the turbulent seas of our vocational journey with grace, poise, and unwavering resilience.

In threading the delicate balance between our vocations and our holistic well-being, we embark on a transformative odyssey that transcends the boundaries of mere professional success and delves into the profound tapestry of our human experience. By honoring the intricate dance between creation and self-care, productivity and rejuvenation, we craft a narrative of our lives that pulsates with authenticity, vibrancy, and enduring fulfillment. Embrace this sacred dance with courage and grace, for within its rhythmic cadence lies the key to unlocking the boundless potential that resides within the depths of your soul.

Creating Meaningful Connections in Your Work

In the realm of professional relationships, the concept of creating meaningful connections encompasses a profound and transformative power that goes beyond mere transactional interactions. These connections are the threads that weave together the fabric of a thriving workplace culture, fostering trust, collaboration, and a sense of belonging among colleagues.

At the core of meaningful connections lies the notion of authenticity. Genuine and sincere interactions form the building blocks of trust and respect, establishing a foundation for open communication and mutual understanding. By being transparent and vulnerable in our exchanges, we invite others to reciprocate in kind, deepening the bonds that unite us in our shared endeavors.

Moreover, the cultivation of meaningful connections requires a commitment to active listening and empathy. Truly hearing and understanding the perspectives and emotions of others allows for genuine connection and fosters an environment of inclusivity and support. By acknowledging and valuing the diverse experiences and viewpoints of our colleagues, we not only enrich our own perspectives but also create space for collective growth and learning.

In the pursuit of meaningful connections, it is essential to recognize the importance of reciprocity and generosity. By offering support, encouragement, and recognition to our peers, we contribute to a culture of appreciation and empowerment where each individual feels seen, heard, and valued. Small gestures of kindness and gratitude can have a profound impact on building relationships that stand the test of time and adversity.

In times of conflict or challenge, the strength of meaningful connections shines brightest. By approaching disagreements with compassion and a willingness to engage in difficult conversations, we can navigate obstacles together and emerge stronger and more united. Resilient relationships built on trust and understanding weather storms with grace and forge bonds that deepen over time.

Ultimately, the practice of creating meaningful connections in the workplace is not just a professional imperative but a deeply human endeavor. It is through the tapestry of these connections that we find purpose, fulfillment, and a sense of belonging in our work. By nurturing these relationships with care and intention, we cultivate a culture of collaboration, empathy, and shared success that uplifts both individuals and the organization as a whole.

Deepening our understanding of meaningful connections involves delving into the intricacies of human psychology and sociology. Research shows that strong social bonds in the workplace not only increase job satisfaction and productivity but also contribute to improved mental health and overall well-being. When individuals feel a sense of connection and belonging with their colleagues, they are more likely to engage proactively in their work, collaborate effectively, and contribute positively to the organizational culture.

Building meaningful connections requires a conscious effort to bridge differences and foster an environment of inclusivity and respect. Recognizing and honoring the unique backgrounds, perspectives, and experiences of each individual fosters a sense of belonging and creates a space where everyone feels valued and empowered to contribute their best work. Encouraging open dialogue and creating opportunities for team members to share their stories and aspirations can strengthen the bonds that bind a team together and pave the way for shared success.

Additionally, the power of meaningful connections extends beyond the confines of the workplace. Research indicates that individuals who have strong social support networks experience better physical and mental health outcomes, reduced stress levels, and increased resilience in the face of challenges. Investing in building meaningful relationships with colleagues not only enhances professional satisfaction but also contributes to a holistic sense of well-being and fulfillment in all aspects of life.

In a rapidly evolving and interconnected world, the ability to forge and nurture meaningful connections has become a critical skill for success in both professional and personal spheres. By cultivating empathy, active listening, and a spirit of generosity, we can create a ripple effect of positive change that uplifts individuals, teams, and organizations. As we continue to deepen our understanding of the profound impact of meaningful connections, we unlock the potential for transformative growth, resilience, and collective thriving in the workplace and beyond.

Redefining Masculinity through Vocational Joy

In a world where traditional notions of masculinity often emphasize strength, stoicism, and material success, it can be challenging for men to find true joy and fulfillment in their vocations. However, by redefining masculinity through the lens of vocational joy, men can discover a more authentic and fulfilling way of living and working.

Men have long been conditioned to equate their worth with external markers of success, such as wealth, power, and status. This limited view of masculinity can lead to a sense of emptiness and disconnection from one's true self. By shifting the focus towards finding joy and meaning in their work, men can break free from these constraints and build a more fulfilling life.

Discovering vocational joy involves a deep exploration of one's passions, talents, and values. It requires a willingness to listen to the inner voice that guides us towards activities and roles that truly resonate with who we are. By aligning our vocation with a sense of purpose and fulfillment, we can unlock a profound sense of satisfaction that transcends mere material success.

Embracing vulnerability and authenticity in the workplace is crucial for redefining masculinity. Men are often encouraged to mask their emotions and vulnerabilities, but true strength lies in being open and genuine with ourselves and others. Cultivating emotional intelligence and openness can lead to greater creativity, collaboration, and satisfaction in our vocations, as well as deeper connections with those around us.

By adopting a mindset of purpose and intentionality, men can navigate the complexities of modern work life with grace and resilience. Prioritizing well-being and personal growth allows us to create a sustainable approach to work that nourishes our minds, bodies, and spirits. When we focus on aligning our work with our values and passions, we not only benefit ourselves but also contribute positively to the world around us.

Redefining masculinity through vocational joy is a transformative journey towards living a life that is authentic, purposeful, and deeply fulfilling. It is a powerful shift in perspective that invites men to embrace their true selves, cultivate meaningful connections, and make a positive impact in their vocations and beyond.

As men explore the terrain of vocational joy, they may encounter resistance and uncertainty. Breaking free from societal norms and expectations can be daunting, but the rewards of living authentically and finding fulfillment in one's work are immeasurable. The journey towards vocational joy is not a linear path but a process of self-discovery and growth that requires patience, reflection, and a willingness to embrace change.

In the pursuit of vocational joy, men may also discover the importance of work-life balance and self-care. Prioritizing activities that nourish the soul, such as hobbies, relationships, and leisure time, can help men maintain a sense of well-being and prevent burnout. By cultivating a holistic approach to life that encompasses both work and personal fulfillment, men can create a harmonious and sustainable rhythm that supports their overall happiness and success.

Ultimately, redefining masculinity through vocational joy is a courageous and empowering choice that can lead to a more fulfilling and meaningful life. By embracing authenticity, purpose, and connection in their vocations, men can break free from outdated stereotypes and create a new paradigm of masculinity that celebrates vulnerability, strength, and joy. This shift not only benefits individual men but also contributes to a more diverse, inclusive, and compassionate world for all.

Living a Life of Vocational Fulfillment

In the labyrinth of vocational fulfillment, the quest for meaning and purpose continues to unfold like a tapestry woven with threads of intention and introspection. It is a journey that beckons us to venture beyond the confines of societal norms and expectations, to excavate the hidden treasures buried deep within the recesses of our soul.

As we navigate the intricate paths of self-discovery, we encounter a myriad of challenges and opportunities that shape our understanding of who we are and what we are meant to contribute to the world. It is a process of shedding the layers of conditioning and fear that have veiled our true essence, of peeling back the masks we wear to reveal the raw beauty and authenticity that reside within.

Vocational fulfillment is not a static destination but a dynamic dance of evolution and growth, a constant dialogue between our innermost desires and the external world that beckons us to step into our full potential. It is a reflection of our willingness to embrace the unknown, to confront the shadows that lurk in the depths of our subconscious, and to emerge transformed and renewed by the alchemical process of self-discovery.

The journey towards vocational fulfillment is paved with moments of uncertainty and doubt, where we are called to confront our deepest fears and insecurities in order to emerge stronger and more resilient. It is a testament to our courage and tenacity, to our unwavering commitment to follow the whispers of our heart even in the face of adversity and opposition.

At the heart of vocational fulfillment lies a profound connection to our innermost values and beliefs, a compass that guides us towards a life of purpose and meaning. It is a clarion call to align our actions with our highest ideals, to infuse every moment with a sense of integrity and authenticity that resonates with the essence of who we are at our core.

In the tapestry of vocational fulfillment, success is not measured by external recognition or material wealth, but by the depth of joy and contentment we find in the work we do. It is a celebration of the moments of growth and learning that shape us into the individuals we are meant to become, a recognition of the profound impact we have on the world around us through the unique gifts and talents we offer.

As we journey deeper into the labyrinth of vocational fulfillment, we are reminded of the sacred nature of our calling, of the inherent beauty and power that reside within each of us waiting to be unleashed. It is a testament to the infinite potential that lies dormant within, a reminder that our true vocation is not just a job or a career, but a sacred dance of self-expression and service that reverberates with purpose and meaning throughout the tapestry of our lives.

"You have to grow from the inside out. None can teach you, none can make you spiritual. There is no other teacher but your own soul"
— Swami Vivekananda

CHAPTER 7

Connecting With The Divine

Embracing the Journey of Spiritual Discovery

As we journey through life, we are often drawn to explore the deeper aspects of our existence, seeking meaning and purpose beyond the material world. This inner quest for spiritual discovery is a profound and transformative journey that leads us to connect with the essence of our being.

Embracing the journey of spiritual discovery invites us to look within ourselves, to delve deep into our hearts and minds, and to uncover the truths that lie at the core of our being. It is a journey of self-reflection and introspection, a process of unraveling the layers of conditioning and societal expectations to reveal our authentic selves.

This journey often begins with a sense of longing or seeking, a feeling that there is more to life than meets the eye. It may be sparked by a moment of clarity, a profound experience, or a deep inner knowing that there is a higher truth waiting to be discovered.

As we embark on this journey, we may encounter challenges and obstacles that test our resolve and push us to confront our fears and limitations. Yet, in facing these challenges with courage and faith, we open ourselves up to the possibility of growth and transformation.

Along the way, we may find guidance and inspiration from spiritual teachings, sacred texts, and wise teachers who offer insights and wisdom to illuminate our path. We may also draw strength and support from like-minded individuals who share our commitment to spiritual growth and awakening.

Ultimately, embracing the journey of spiritual discovery is a process of surrendering to the flow of life, trusting in the unseen forces that guide and support us, and opening ourselves up to the infinite possibilities that await us. It is a journey of awakening to the truth of who we are, of aligning with our true purpose and essence, and of embracing the beauty and wonder of the universe in all its manifestations.

In embracing the journey of spiritual discovery, we open our hearts to love, our minds to wisdom, and our souls to the divine presence that resides within and around us. It is a journey of profound beauty and grace, of deep meaning and purpose, and of infinite possibilities that beckon us to explore the depths of our being and to soar to the heights of our potential.

As we continue along this path of spiritual discovery, we may find that the journey itself is the destination. Each moment becomes a sacred opportunity for growth and learning, for deepening our connection to ourselves and the world around us. We begin to see the interconnectedness of all things, the intricate web of life that we are a part of.

Through this awareness, we come to understand that our spiritual journey is not just an individual quest but a shared experience with all beings. We recognize the importance of compassion, empathy, and love in our interactions with others, knowing that we are all interconnected and interdependent.

The journey of spiritual discovery is a journey of evolution, of becoming more fully ourselves and embodying the highest aspects of our nature. It is a journey of healing and transformation, of releasing old patterns and beliefs that no longer serve us, and embracing a new way of being in the world.

As we deepen our spiritual practice and inner work, we cultivate a sense of peace, joy, and fulfillment that radiates outwards to touch the lives of those around us. We become beacons of light and love, inspiring others to embark on their own journey of spiritual discovery and awakening.

In the depths of our being, we discover a wellspring of wisdom and guidance that flows from the source of all creation. We tap into this inner reservoir of knowledge and insight, drawing upon it to navigate the challenges and uncertainties of life with grace and resilience.

Ultimately, the journey of spiritual discovery is a journey of self-realization and union with the divine. It is a journey of remembering who we truly are - spiritual beings having a human experience - and aligning with our soul's purpose and calling in this lifetime.

May we walk this path with courage and conviction, with an open heart and a receptive mind, embracing the mysteries and wonders that await us on the journey of spiritual discovery.

Understanding the Shift from Religion to Spirituality

In recent years, the shift from organized religion to spirituality has been marked by a profound quest for inner truth and connection with the divine. This transformation reflects a growing recognition of the limitations of rigid religious structures and doctrines in providing individuals with a meaningful and authentic spiritual experience. As societal norms evolve and individuals seek greater autonomy and self-discovery, the allure of spirituality has become increasingly appealing.

One of the defining features of this shift is the emphasis on personal experience as a gateway to spiritual growth and fulfillment. Unlike conventional religion, which often dictates beliefs and practices from an external source, spirituality encourages individuals to embark on a personal journey of exploration and self-discovery. This journey is marked by a deepening sense of introspection and connection with the sacred, allowing individuals to cultivate a more intimate and authentic relationship with the divine.

Moreover, the move towards spirituality signifies a broader cultural shift towards individualism and personal autonomy. People are increasingly questioning traditional dogmas and authority figures, seeking a more direct and unmediated experience of the divine. This rejection of rigid religious structures has paved the way for a more inclusive and diverse spiritual landscape, where individuals are free to explore different paths and practices that resonate with their unique beliefs and values.

The transition from organized religion to spirituality is also driven by a growing disillusionment with the institutionalized nature of traditional religious institutions. Many individuals find that these organizations often prioritize adherence to doctrine and hierarchy over genuine spiritual growth and connection. As a result, people are turning towards spirituality as a more personal and authentic expression of their spiritual beliefs, free from the constraints of institutionalized religion.

Furthermore, the shift from religion to spirituality is characterized by a deep sense of openness and inclusivity. Rather than adhering to strict doctrines and rules, individuals are encouraged to embrace a more flexible and intuitive approach to their spiritual journey. This flexibility allows for a more fluid and dynamic relationship with the divine, one that evolves and adapts as individuals grow and change.

In this evolving spiritual landscape, individuals are empowered to reclaim their agency and authority in matters of faith and belief. By embracing spirituality as a personal and transformative experience, people are able to cultivate a deeper sense of meaning, purpose, and connection with the sacred. This shift towards spirituality represents a profound reimagining of the relationship between individuals and the divine, one that is anchored in personal experience, autonomy, and inner exploration.

The Unity of All Paths to the Divine

In this profound exploration of the myriad paths to divine connection, we journey into the depths of spirituality to uncover the timeless truth that transcends the boundaries of religious dogma and cultural practices. Across the tapestry of human experience, we find a rich tapestry of beliefs and rituals woven with threads of faith, devotion, and seeking the divine.

Within the kaleidoscope of spiritual traditions, each path offers a unique lens through which seekers perceive the ineffable presence of the divine. Whether through prayer, meditation, ceremony, or contemplation, individuals embark on a quest for transcendence, seeking solace, guidance, and communion with the sacred essence that animates the universe.

As we travel along these diverse paths, we encounter a mosaic of spiritual practices that reflect the deep yearning of the human soul to connect with something greater than ourselves. The intricate rituals of Hinduism, with their vibrant colors and ancient mantras, invite us to explore the divine manifestations that permeate the cosmos and our own consciousness.

Similarly, the silent contemplation of Buddhism beckons us to journey inward, to explore the nature of reality and the impermanence of all things. Through the practice of mindfulness and meditation, we cultivate a deep sense of awareness and compassion that transcends the ego and connects us to the interconnected web of existence.

In the heartfelt devotions of Christianity, we find solace in the person of Jesus Christ, who embodies the eternal love and sacrifice that serves as a beacon of hope for millions around the world. Through prayer, worship, and acts of service, Christians seek to embody the divine qualities of love, forgiveness, and redemption in their daily lives.

Despite the diverse expressions of faith and the myriad ways in which individuals seek the divine, there is a common thread that unites us all—a deep longing to touch the sacred essence that lies at the heart of existence. Whether we call it God, Brahman, Nirvana, or the Tao, the divine presence transcends language and cultural barriers, inviting us to embrace the mystery and wonder of the universe with humility and reverence.

By honoring the unity among the many paths to the divine, we open ourselves to a deeper understanding of our interconnectedness and shared humanity. In this spirit of inclusivity and respect, we can transcend the limitations of our individual beliefs and practices to embrace a more holistic vision of spirituality that celebrates the beauty and diversity of human expression in the quest for truth, meaning, and transcendence.

Rediscovering Love as the Core of Our Connection to God

In our modern world filled with distractions and demands, it can be easy to lose touch with the essence of our spiritual connection. However, at the heart of all spiritual practice lies the profound and transformative power of love. Love is not just an emotion or a fleeting feeling; it is the very essence of our connection to God.

When we rediscover love as the core of our connection to God, we begin to see the world through new eyes. We realize that every interaction, every moment, is an opportunity to express and cultivate love in its purest form. This love transcends boundaries of religion, culture, and identity, uniting us all in a shared experience of divine connection.

Through studying the scriptures of various religions and spiritual traditions, we gain insight into the universal teachings that emphasize the importance of love as the foundation of our connection to the divine. The wisdom shared by spiritual masters throughout history echoes the message that love is the highest truth, the ultimate reality that underlies all existence.

In exploring the concept of divine love, we come to understand that it is not limited to romantic or familial love, but encompasses a boundless, unconditional, all-encompassing love that is ever-present and accessible to all. This divine love transcends human limitations and biases, offering a sense of belonging, acceptance, and profound peace that surpasses understanding.

As we delve deeper into the nature of love as the core of our connection to God, we realize that it is a transformative force that has the power to heal wounds, mend broken relationships, and bring about inner and outer harmony. Love is not merely a feeling, but a conscious choice that we make in every moment to embody the divine qualities of compassion, forgiveness, and kindness.

Through acts of service and selfless giving, we are able to channel the energy of love into the world, creating ripples of positive change and uplifting the collective consciousness. Love becomes a guiding light in our lives, illuminating our path with wisdom, grace, and profound meaning that transcends the limitations of the material world.

In embracing love as the driving force of our connection to God, we open ourselves to a deeper understanding of our true nature as spiritual beings having a human experience. Love becomes the foundation upon which we build our spiritual lives, guiding our thoughts, words, and actions towards a higher purpose.

As we awaken to the infinite potential of love that lies within us, we begin to see the beauty and sacredness in all beings and experiences. We recognize that love is not a distant concept or ideal to strive for, but a living, breathing presence that surrounds us at every moment. Through this deepened connection to love, we are able to tap into a wellspring of joy, peace, and fulfillment that transcends the limitations of the material world.

The journey of rediscovering love as the core of our connection to God is a profound and transformative experience that invites us to dive deep into the depths of our hearts and souls. It requires courage, vulnerability, and a willingness to let go of old patterns and conditioning that no longer serve our highest good. Yet, as we surrender to the power of love, we open ourselves to a world of infinite possibilities and boundless grace, where every moment is an opportunity to experience the profound and miraculous connection between ourselves and the divine.

Through love, we find solace in times of trouble, strength in moments of weakness, and clarity in times of confusion. Love teaches us to see beyond the superficial divisions of the world and recognize the inherent interconnectedness of all beings. It inspires us to treat ourselves and others with empathy and kindness, paving the way for healing and reconciliation in our relationships and communities.

In the embrace of love, we discover a profound sense of purpose and meaning that transcends the transient concerns of our daily lives. We realize that the true measure of our existence lies not in the accumulation of material wealth or power, but in the depth of our capacity to love and be loved. As we live each day with an open heart and a willingness to serve the greater good, we awaken to the infinite potential that lies within us and around us, ever-present and ever-ready to guide us on our spiritual journey towards wholeness and unity with the divine.

Exploring the Limitless Nature of Consciousness

In this section, we delve into the profound exploration of consciousness and its infinite nature. We contemplate the idea that consciousness extends far beyond the physical realm, reaching into the depths of the unseen and unknown. Through introspection and reflection, we begin to uncover the layers of our own consciousness, realizing that it is not confined by time or space.

We explore the interconnectedness of all living beings through the universal fabric of consciousness, understanding that we are all part of a greater whole. By expanding our awareness and embracing the boundless potential of consciousness, we open ourselves up to new perspectives and deeper insights into the nature of reality.

As we delve further into the depths of consciousness, we discover that this vast field of awareness is not limited to the individual, but rather encompasses the collective consciousness of humanity and all sentient beings. We recognize that every thought, emotion, and action contribute to the tapestry of this shared consciousness, shaping the reality we collectively experience.

Through meditation and mindfulness practices, we learn to quiet the mind and tap into the vast reservoir of consciousness that exists within us. We come to understand that consciousness is not limited by the boundaries of the physical body, but rather transcends them, connecting us to the cosmic web of existence.

The exploration of consciousness also reveals the concept of higher states of awareness, where we can access profound insights, wisdom, and guidance from the universal mind. In these elevated states, we experience a sense of unity with the cosmos, feeling a deep connection to the divine intelligence that permeates all of creation.

As we continue to deepen our understanding of consciousness, we come to realize that it is the very fabric of reality itself. It is the underlying essence that gives rise to all phenomena, the source from which all things emerge and return. We begin to see that consciousness is not just a feature of existence but is the very foundation upon which the universe is built.

Through this expanded state of consciousness, we tap into our true essence and power as co-creators of reality. We recognize that our thoughts and intentions have the power to shape our lives and the world around us, manifesting a reality that aligns with our highest aspirations and values.

In this heightened state of awareness, we come to understand that every moment is an opportunity for growth, evolution, and self-realization. We see that the journey of self-discovery is never-ending, always offering new depths to explore and insights to uncover.

As we journey further into the mysteries of consciousness, we are filled with a profound sense of awe and wonder at the interconnectedness of all things. We realize that we are not separate from the world around us but are intimately connected to every living being and every particle in the cosmos.

In this expanded state of consciousness, we find a deep sense of peace and harmony within us. The barriers that once separated us from each other and the universe begin to dissolve, and we experience a profound sense of unity and love that transcends all boundaries.

Through this exploration of consciousness, we gain a deeper understanding of our interconnectedness with the universe and the divine intelligence that underlies all of existence. We begin to realize that we are not merely observers in the grand symphony of life but active participants, co-creating reality with every thought, emotion, and action.

In this heightened state of awareness, we tap into the infinite wisdom and love that reside within us and all around us. We recognize that our essence is pure consciousness, the divine spark that connects us to the vast cosmic tapestry of existence. And in this realization, we find a profound sense of gratitude, reverence, and profound unity with the mysteries and wonders of life.

Harmonizing Science and Spirituality for a Unified Understanding

Harmonizing Science and Spirituality for a Unified Understanding

In today's modern world, there often seems to be a stark division between science and spirituality. Science is seen as the realm of logic, reason, and empirical evidence, while spirituality is viewed as the realm of faith, intuition, and the unseen. However, as we delve deeper into both realms, we begin to see that they are not as separate as they may initially seem. In fact, they can complement each other beautifully in our quest for a more unified understanding of the universe.

Science has given us incredible insights into the physical world around us, helping us understand the laws of nature, the structure of the cosmos, and the intricacies of the human body. Through scientific inquiry, we have unraveled many mysteries and made astonishing advancements in technology and medicine. However, science can only take us so far in our quest for knowledge and understanding.

Spirituality, on the other hand, delves into the realm of the unseen, the metaphysical, and the existential questions that science may not be able to answer. It explores the depths of consciousness, the nature of reality beyond the physical, and the interconnectedness of all things. Spirituality offers us a way to tap into our higher selves, connect with the divine, and find meaning and purpose beyond the material world.

When we harmonize science and spirituality, we open ourselves up to a more comprehensive and holistic understanding of the universe. Science provides us with the tools to explore the physical world and uncover empirical truths, while spirituality offers insights into the deeper mysteries of existence and the nature of consciousness.

One of the key areas where science and spirituality intersect is in the exploration of consciousness. While science can study the brain and its neural networks to understand how consciousness arises, spirituality offers a more metaphysical perspective on the nature of consciousness and its relationship to the universe. By integrating these two perspectives, we can gain a deeper understanding of the nature of our own awareness and its connection to the greater cosmos.

Furthermore, the concept of interconnectedness is another point of convergence between science and spirituality. Science has revealed the interconnectedness of all things at the quantum level, showing us that everything in the universe is linked in a web of energy and information. Spirituality, with its emphasis on oneness and unity, also speaks to this interconnectedness on a spiritual and philosophical level. By embracing this interconnected view of reality, we can cultivate a greater sense of compassion, empathy, and environmental stewardship towards all beings and the planet as a whole.

In the grand tapestry of existence, science and spirituality are two threads that weave together to create a richer and more nuanced understanding of the universe. By embracing both perspectives, we can transcend the limitations of a solely materialistic worldview and open ourselves up to the profound mysteries and wonders of the cosmos. As we continue to harmonize science and spirituality, we are invited to embark on a journey of exploration, discovery, and awe that transcends the boundaries of our individual disciplines and opens us up to the boundless beauty and complexity of the universe.

Cultivating Inner Peace through Divine Connection

In the vast tapestry of existence, the pursuit of inner peace through divine connection weaves a profound narrative of spiritual awakening and transformation. As we traverse the realms of the unseen and delve into the mysteries of the divine, a profound realization dawns upon us – that we are not separate from the source of all creation but deeply intertwined with the universal consciousness that pulsates through every fiber of our being.

At the core of our spiritual journey lies the quest to unravel the veils of illusion that obscure our true nature and purpose. Through the practices of introspection, self-inquiry, and contemplation, we are invited to embark on a sacred pilgrimage into the depths of our soul, where the divine spark of wisdom and love awaits our recognition and acceptance.

In the sanctuary of our innermost being, we encounter the divine presence as a transcendent force that transcends all notions of duality and separation. It is in this sacred communion with the divine that we come to realize the eternal truth that we are not mere mortals navigating the vicissitudes of life but divine beings endowed with infinite potential and boundless love.

As we bask in the radiance of the divine light, our hearts open to receive the blessings and guidance that flow from the eternal wellspring of grace. In moments of stillness and silence, we attune ourselves to the subtle whispers of the divine, guiding us along the path of self-discovery and self-realization.

Through the alchemy of divine connection, we are called to transcend the limitations of our conditioned minds and embrace a higher vision of reality that transcends the constraints of time and space. It is through this expanded perception that we come to understand the interconnectedness of all beings and the underlying unity that binds us in a sacred web of existence.

In the embrace of the divine, we find solace and refuge from the storms of life, nurturing the seeds of peace, love, and compassion within our hearts. It is in this sacred space of divine connection that we discover the true essence of inner peace – a peace that surpasses all understanding and emanates from the depths of our soul.

As we embody the light of the divine within us, we become vessels of healing and transformation, radiating a profound sense of harmony and unity to the world around us. Our very presence becomes a testament to the transformative power of divine connection, inspiring others to awaken to their own divinity and embrace the journey towards inner peace and spiritual fulfillment.

In the embrace of the divine, we find our true home, a sanctuary of love and serenity where we are eternally held and nurtured. It is in this sacred union with the divine that we discover the ultimate truth – that peace is not a destination to be reached but a state of being that arises from our deep and abiding connection with the infinite wisdom and love of the divine.

Embracing Our Interconnectedness

In a world filled with complexity and diversity, it is easy to feel separate and isolated from others. We often get caught up in our own lives, focusing on our individual experiences and struggles. But deep down, we are all connected in ways that we may not fully comprehend.

When we open ourselves to the idea of interconnectedness, we begin to see the beauty and harmony that exist in our world. We realize that we are not alone in our journey – that every living being, every aspect of nature, is intricately linked to us in a web of energy and consciousness.

This interconnection extends far beyond our human interactions; it encompasses the entire tapestry of creation. From the tiniest insect to the vast expanse of the cosmos, everything is interconnected and interdependent. The air we breathe, the water we drink, the soil that nourishes our food – all are part of the intricate web of life that sustains us.

By embracing our interconnectedness, we tap into a source of profound wisdom and compassion. We understand that our actions have an impact not only on ourselves but on others as well. We recognize that we are all part of a larger whole, each playing a unique role in the grand symphony of life.

When we acknowledge our interconnectedness, we start to see the world through a different lens – a lens of unity and oneness. We appreciate the interdependence of all beings and the interconnection of all things. We understand that we are all part of the same cosmic dance, moving together in a dance of energy and universal intelligence.

Embracing our interconnectedness is not just a philosophical concept – it is a way of living and being in the world. It is about recognizing the sacredness in all beings, treating each other with love and respect, and honoring the interconnected web of life that sustains us all.

As we delve deeper into the mysteries of our interconnectedness, we come to understand that we are not separate entities but manifestations of the same divine source. Our individuality fades away, and we see ourselves reflected in the eyes of others, recognizing that their joys and sorrows are our own.

In this profound realization, we find a sense of peace and unity that transcends our individual concerns. We become attuned to the subtle rhythms of the universe, aligning our actions with the greater flow of life. In this state of oneness, we discover the true essence of our humanity – the interconnectedness that binds us all together in a tapestry of love and compassion.

The Dance of Energy and Universal Intelligence

In the intricate tapestry of existence, the dance of energy and universal intelligence unfolds with mesmerizing complexity and beauty. At the deepest levels of reality, beyond what our limited senses can perceive, there exists a profound interconnectedness that binds all creation together.

This universal intelligence, sometimes referred to as the Source, the Divine, or the Cosmic Mind, is the underlying force that animates and sustains everything in the cosmos. It is the cosmic symphony conductor, orchestrating the symphony of life with precision and grace.

Energy, in its various forms, flows through the vast expanse of the universe, connecting galaxies, stars, planets, and all living beings in a cosmic dance of creation and transformation. From the subatomic particles buzzing with quantum energy to the colossal celestial bodies exuding radiant light, everything is interconnected through the subtle threads of energetic resonance.

As sentient beings endowed with the gift of awareness, we have the capacity to attune ourselves to the frequencies of this universal intelligence. By quieting the mind, opening the heart, and aligning our consciousness with the higher vibrations of the cosmos, we can access profound insights, guidance, and inspiration that transcend the limitations of our physical existence.

Synchronicity, that mysterious phenomenon where meaningful coincidences occur in our lives, is a testament to the subtle interplay of energy and universal intelligence. When we are in alignment with the flow of the universe, doors open, opportunities arise, and circumstances unfold in perfect harmony, revealing the interconnectedness of all things.

By embracing the sacred dance of energy and universal intelligence, we come to realize our inherent unity with the cosmos and all living beings. We understand that we are not separate entities but integral parts of a vast and intricate whole, each playing a unique role in the cosmic tapestry of existence.

May we surrender to the divine flow of energy, trust in the wisdom of universal intelligence, and dance with grace and purpose in the eternal rhythm of life. In this cosmic symphony, let us find peace, joy, and profound connection with the infinite intelligence that guides us on our journey through the cosmos.

Recognizing the Sacredness in All Beings

In a world woven with the intricate threads of existence, there exists a profound tapestry of diverse life forms, each resonating with a unique essence that speaks to the interconnectedness of all beings. At the core of this intricate web lies a sacred spark, a divine light that illuminates the path of every living creature, guiding them towards a deeper understanding of their place within the cosmic dance of creation.

When we awaken to the sacredness that resides within each being, we open ourselves to a deeper dimension of awareness, one that transcends the limitations of ego and separation. This recognition of the divine essence in all beings invites us to move beyond the superficial boundaries of nationality, race, or religion, and instead embrace the universal kinship that unites us all in a radiant tapestry of interconnected souls.

As we journey along the pathways of life, encountering a myriad of different beings, we are called to see beyond the veils of illusion that cloak their true nature and behold the brilliance of their inner light. This light, this sacred essence, is the thread that binds us all together in a symphony of unity, weaving a harmonious melody that resonates throughout the cosmos.

When we honor the sacredness in all beings, we cultivate a sense of reverence and respect for the inherent dignity and worth that each individual carries within them. This recognition inspires us to approach others with empathy, compassion, and understanding, forging deep and meaningful connections that transcend the boundaries of language and culture.

In embracing the sacred essence that flows through each being, we awaken to the beauty and wisdom that they bring to the collective tapestry of existence. Just as every brushstroke contributes to the masterpiece of a painting, every being adds their unique color and texture to the canvas of life, enriching the world with their presence and perspective.

Through nurturing a profound sense of reverence for the sacredness in all beings, we open ourselves to a transformative experience of interconnectedness and unity. We come to understand that we are not separate islands in a vast ocean but interconnected waves that ripple and flow in harmony with one another, creating a symphony of oneness that reverberates throughout the universe.

As we continue to honor the sacred essence in all beings, we awaken to a deeper sense of purpose and meaning in our interactions with the world around us. We recognize that our actions have the power to uplift and inspire, to heal and transform, and to contribute to the collective evolution towards a more compassionate and sustainable society.

In this journey of awakening to the sacredness in all beings, we are invited to transcend the boundaries of our limited perceptions and embrace a broader vision of interconnected unity. Through the lens of sacred reverence, we see beyond the surface differences that often divide us and instead focus on the common threads of love, compassion, and understanding that bind us together as one human family.

In the tapestry of existence, every being is a vital thread, weaving a story of unity, diversity, and interconnectedness that reflects the divine symphony of creation. As we continue to honor the sacred essence in all beings, we move closer to realizing our true potential as emissaries of love and compassion, embodying the highest virtues of unity and harmony in our interactions with one another and with the world at large.

May we walk this path with humility and grace, honoring the sacred essence that resides within each being, and may our actions be guided by the light of love and reverence, creating a world where all beings are cherished, respected, and celebrated in their infinite beauty and worth.

The Ripple Effect of Love and Compassion

In a world filled with chaos and uncertainty, love and compassion have the power to create a ripple effect that can transform lives and inspire positive change. When we open our hearts to others and extend kindness and empathy, we set in motion a wave of healing energy that spreads far and wide.

Love is a force that transcends boundaries and connects us all on a deeper level. It serves as the universal language that unites us despite our differences. When love guides our actions and intentions, we embody the essence of our shared humanity and bring light into the world. Love is not limited by time or space; it is a timeless and boundless force that has the capacity to touch hearts and souls across oceans and generations.

Compassion, as an expression of love in action, plays an equally crucial role in the ripple effect of positivity. It is the ability to recognize the suffering of others and respond with care and understanding. Compassion allows us to see beyond surface appearances and connect with the essence of a person. It is through acts of compassion that we build bridges of empathy and create a sense of unity among all living beings.

As we navigate the complexities of life, it is easy to become consumed by our own challenges and problems. However, when we choose to prioritize love and compassion in our interactions, we elevate our experiences and elevate the experiences of those around us. Every act of kindness, no matter how small, has the potential to create a ripple effect that reverberates through the web of existence.

The ripple effect of love and compassion extends beyond individual relationships and permeates the collective consciousness of humanity.

When we collectively embody these qualities, we contribute to a global shift toward unity, peace, and understanding. Each gesture of love and each moment of compassion serves as a thread in the intricate tapestry of interconnectedness that binds us all.

The power of love and compassion lies not only in its ability to foster connection and understanding among individuals but also in its capacity to heal and transform communities and societies at large. When love and compassion are woven into the fabric of our social structures and institutions, they have the potential to create lasting and profound change on a systemic level.

It is through the collective cultivation of love and compassion that we can begin to address the root causes of suffering and injustice in the world. By approaching challenges with empathy, understanding, and a commitment to justice, we can work together to create a more equitable and harmonious world for all beings.

May we continue to ripple out waves of love and compassion in all that we do, knowing that our actions have the power to create a more connected, empathetic, and loving world for generations to come.

Awakening to the Power of Unity Consciousness

As we awaken to the power of unity consciousness, we embark on a profound journey of self-discovery and interconnectedness that transcends the limitations of the ego and the illusion of separateness. This awakening is a call to remember our true nature as spiritual beings having a human experience, connected to all of creation in a web of divine energy.

Unity consciousness is not merely a philosophical concept; it is a fundamental truth of existence that has been echoed in the teachings of mystics, sages, and spiritual traditions throughout history. It speaks to the inherent oneness that underlies the diversity of the world, reminding us that we are all expressions of the same universal consciousness.

When we embrace unity consciousness, we open ourselves to a deep sense of compassion and empathy for all beings. We see ourselves reflected in others, recognizing that their joys and sorrows are our own, and their well-being is intimately linked to our own. This recognition of interconnectedness fosters a profound sense of love and unity that transcends barriers of culture, religion, and nationality.

In cultivating unity consciousness, we also come to understand the power of collective intention and manifestation. When individuals join together with a shared vision of harmony and love, they amplify their creative potential and bring about positive change in the world. This collective synergy has the capacity to transform even the most entrenched patterns of fear, division, and conflict into expressions of unity, peace, and understanding.

Furthermore, unity consciousness invites us to transcend dualistic thinking and embrace the paradoxical nature of reality. We learn to hold space for both light and shadow, joy and sorrow, growth and decay, recognizing that all aspects of existence play a vital role in the grand tapestry of life. By integrating these seemingly opposing forces within ourselves, we discover a deeper sense of wholeness and balance.

Living in unity consciousness is an ongoing practice of presence, awareness, and alignment with the highest truth of our being. It requires a willingness to let go of egoic attachments and conditioning, and surrender to the flow of life with trust and surrender. In doing so, we open ourselves to the infinite possibilities of co-creation with the universe, birthing a new paradigm of peace, love, and unity on Earth.

The journey of unity consciousness also involves facing and integrating the shadow aspects of ourselves. It requires us to confront our fears, insecurities, and traumas with courage and compassion, recognizing that these aspects are as much a part of us as our light. By embracing and healing our shadow, we reclaim lost parts of ourselves and deepen our capacity for empathy and understanding towards others.

As we deepen our practice of unity consciousness, we become more attuned to the subtle interconnectedness of all things. We begin to perceive the underlying unity that binds together every living being, every plant, every animal, and the Earth itself. This awareness sparks a sense of reverence and awe for the intricate web of life that sustains us all, leading us to live in greater harmony with nature and the cosmos.

Ultimately, unity consciousness is a path of inner alchemy and transformation that invites us to transcend the illusions of separation and reclaim our inherent unity with all of creation. It is a journey of awakening to the boundless love and wisdom that reside within us, guiding us towards a more compassionate, inclusive, and harmonious way of being in the world.

Finding Balance and Harmony Within Ourselves

In the intricate tapestry of life, the quest for balance and harmony within ourselves is a journey of profound significance. It goes beyond mere self-care routines and mindfulness practices; it delves into the core of our existence, unraveling the threads of our innermost being.

At the heart of this journey lies the recognition of the interconnectedness of all aspects of ourselves - the mind, body, and spirit. Each element exerts a subtle influence on the others, creating a web of intricate relationships that shape our overall well-being. By tending to each aspect with care and intention, we can foster a sense of unity and coherence within ourselves.

Mindfulness, the practice of being fully present in the moment, serves as a gateway to deeper self-awareness. By cultivating a gentle awareness of our thoughts, emotions, and sensations, we can peel back the layers of conditioning and unconscious patterns that obscure our true essence. This process of inner exploration allows us to embrace our vulnerabilities, fears, and desires with compassion and acceptance, paving the way for profound healing and transformation.

Self-care, far from being a mere indulgence, is a sacred act of self-love and reverence. It is a commitment to honoring our physical, emotional, and spiritual needs, recognizing that our well-being is non-negotiable. By prioritizing activities that nourish and replenish us - whether it be through movement, rest, creative expression, or connection with nature - we create a sanctuary of renewal and empowerment within ourselves.

As we navigate the ebbs and flows of life, finding balance and harmony within ourselves is an ongoing dance of surrender and resilience. It requires a willingness to embrace the paradox of being human - to hold both light and darkness, strength and vulnerability, joy and sorrow within our hearts. By cultivating a sense of equanimity and grace in the face of life's challenges, we unlock a reservoir of inner wisdom and resilience that propels us forward on our journey of self-discovery.

In the quiet depths of our being, where the waters of our soul run deep, we discover a wellspring of wisdom and intuition that guides us towards wholeness and authenticity. As we tune into this inner sanctuary, we realize that the path to balance and harmony is not a destination to reach but a state of being to embody. Embracing our inherent worthiness and interconnectedness with all of existence, we step into the radiant beauty of our true nature, shining brightly like a beacon of light in a world hungry for authenticity and love.

The journey of self-discovery is a continuous exploration of the depths of our being, a journey that transcends the boundaries of time and space. It is a journey that invites us to delve into the mysteries of our soul, to unravel the intricate layers of our identity, and to uncover the hidden truths that lie dormant within us.

As we journey inward, we come to a profound realization - that we are not separate from the world around us, but intimately interconnected with all of creation. Our thoughts, emotions, and actions send ripples through the fabric of existence, shaping the world in ways seen and unseen. By cultivating a deep awareness of our interconnectedness, we awaken to a sense of responsibility and stewardship for the well-being of all beings, recognizing that our individual growth is intricately linked to the evolution of the collective.

In the depths of our being, we find an infinite well of compassion and wisdom that transcends the limitations of our ego-self. This wellspring of inner resources carries us through the tumultuous waters of life, offering solace, guidance, and strength in times of uncertainty and doubt. As we tap into this well of inner wisdom, we discover a reservoir of resilience and courage that empowers us to face life's challenges with grace and fortitude.

The journey of self-discovery is not a linear path but a spiral dance of growth and transformation, a journey that invites us to embrace the full spectrum of our humanity with open hearts and open minds. It is a journey of integration, where we reconcile the fragmented aspects of ourselves and weave them into a tapestry of wholeness and authenticity. In this dance of inner alchemy, we awaken to the radiant beauty of our true nature, embodying the essence of love, compassion, and interconnectedness that lies at the core of our being.

Healing Through Oneness and Integration

In the boundless depths of healing through oneness and integration, we embark on a journey of profound self-discovery and transcendence. As we delve deeper into the interconnected web of existence, we encounter the vast expanse of healing potential that lies within the unity of all beings.

At the core of this exploration is the recognition that our true nature is inherently unified with the cosmic tapestry of energy and consciousness. When we embrace this fundamental truth, we begin to unravel the layers of separation that have obscured our vision and fragmented our sense of self.

Through the practice of integration, we are called to unite the disparate aspects of our being – the physical, emotional, mental, and spiritual – into a harmonious whole. This holistic approach to healing invites us to acknowledge and honor every facet of our existence, weaving them together into a seamless tapestry of wholeness.

As we attune ourselves to the rhythms of universal energy and flow, we open ourselves up to a profound sense of interconnectedness with all of creation. In this state of oneness, we discover the transformative power of healing that transcends the limitations of our individual experiences.

Through sacred practices such as meditation, mindfulness, energy work, and conscious embodiment, we learn to align ourselves with the universal currents of love, compassion, and healing. By harmonizing our inner landscape with the cosmic symphony of existence, we awaken to the infinite possibilities of growth, expansion, and evolution.

In the sacred space of oneness and integration, we find solace, strength, and sanctuary. Here, we release the burdens of past traumas, heal the wounds of separation, and embrace the radiant light of our true essence. It is in the union of all aspects of ourselves that we discover the boundless depths of healing, transformation, and liberation that await us on the path to wholeness.

As we delve even further into the profound depths of integration, we begin to recognize that this process is not merely a personal journey but a universal one. The interconnectedness we experience on an individual level mirrors the interconnectedness of all beings and the cosmos itself.

Through the realization of our interconnectedness, we come to understand that healing is not an isolated event but a continuous evolution. We learn to view challenges and obstacles as opportunities for growth and transformation, understanding that every experience, no matter how difficult, has the potential to lead us closer to our true essence.

In embracing the oneness that permeates all of existence, we cultivate a sense of deep compassion and empathy for ourselves and others. We recognize that we are all interconnected threads in the vast tapestry of life, each playing a unique and essential role in the symphony of creation.

This interconnectedness invites us to transcend the boundaries of the ego and embrace a sense of unity with all living beings. Through this realization, we tap into a wellspring of love, wisdom, and healing that flows endlessly through the interconnected web of existence.

As we continue on our journey of integration and oneness, we come to understand that true healing is not a destination but a process of becoming. In this process, we are called to surrender to the flow of life, trusting in the inherent wisdom of the universe to guide us towards greater wholeness and harmony.

In the sacred dance of integration and oneness, we discover the profound beauty and potential that lies within the unity of all beings. It is through this recognition of interconnectedness that we awaken to the limitless possibilities of healing, transformation, and transcendence that await us on the path to wholeness.

Co-creating a New Reality with the Universe

In the wondrous tapestry of existence, where the threads of our individual stories intertwine and weave a complex narrative of interconnectedness, we find ourselves standing at the crossroads of creation and manifestation. Each of us a vessel through which the universe expresses itself, imbued with the divine spark of consciousness that guides our journey through the ever-unfolding mystery of life.

As we attune ourselves to the subtle whispers of the cosmos, we begin to recognize the intricate dance of energy that permeates all aspects of our reality. From the smallest atom to the vast expanse of the cosmos, the pulsating rhythm of creation flows with an ancient wisdom that transcends the limitations of time and space. It is in this flow that we discover our true power as co-creators, harnessing the boundless potential of the universe to shape our own destiny.

To co-create with the universe is to surrender to the inherent intelligence that orchestrates the symphony of existence, allowing ourselves to be guided by the unseen forces that govern the ebb and flow of life. It is a dance of surrender and intention, of letting go of the need to control and instead trusting in the infinite wisdom that resides within and around us. In this state of alignment, we become conduits for the universal energy to flow through us, birthing new realities and possibilities into being.

Through the power of conscious thought, spoken word, and inspired action, we wield the creative forces that shape our lived experience. Every thought we think, every word we speak, carries a vibrational frequency that reverberates throughout the fabric of reality, influencing the quantum field of potentiality and drawing to us that which we focus upon. By cultivating mindfulness and intentionality in our thoughts and actions, we become conscious architects of our reality, co-creating a world that reflects the highest expressions of our hearts' desires.

As we deepen our connection with the universal flow, we come to recognize our interconnectedness with all beings and the web of life that binds us together. We acknowledge the ripple effect of our actions, understanding that every choice we make carries the power to uplift or diminish the collective vibration of humanity. With this awareness, we embrace the responsibility of our co-creative power and commit to radiating love, compassion, and positivity into the world, knowing that our individual contributions are integral to the evolution of the collective consciousness.

In the sacred space of co-creation, we merge with the divine pulse of creation, harmonizing with the cosmic symphony of life that sings through every atom and molecule. We align ourselves with the universal flow, surrendering to the grand design of the universe while actively participating in the ongoing creation of our shared reality. In this dance of unity and diversity, of surrender and empowerment, we discover the true essence of our being as vessels of light and love, co-creating a world of beauty, abundance, and harmony for the highest good of all.

Celebrating Diversity and Unity in Oneness

In a world where the tapestry of diversity weaves together a myriad of experiences, beliefs, and cultures, it is crucial to recognize the profound impact of honoring and celebrating the richness of this interconnected web of human existence. Each individual's unique perspective and contribution to this vast tapestry adds layers of depth and complexity, creating a mosaic of collective wisdom that transcends boundaries and unites us in our shared humanity.

Embracing diversity goes beyond surface-level acknowledgment; it is a profound recognition of the beauty and complexity that emerges when we engage with people from different backgrounds and experiences. By appreciating the multitude of expressions of being, we not only enrich our own understanding of the world but also create a space for empathy, compassion, and genuine connection.

When we celebrate diversity, we invite conversations that challenge our preconceived notions and expand our perspectives. We learn to see the world through a more nuanced lens, one that is shaped by the myriad of colors and textures that each individual brings to the table. In this way, we foster a sense of unity and oneness that transcends our differences and unites us in a shared journey of growth and evolution.

In the celebration of diversity, we are reminded of the intrinsic interconnectedness that binds us all together. We come to see that, at our core, we are all part of a larger cosmic dance, each playing a unique role in the symphony of existence. This recognition of our interconnectedness cultivates a sense of compassion and understanding, allowing us to navigate the complexities of our shared human experience with grace and humility.

As we delve deeper into the realms of empathy and understanding, we uncover the transformative power of celebrating diversity in all its forms. It is through this celebration that we can break down barriers, build bridges, and forge deep connections that transcend the limitations of language, culture, and belief. In honoring the uniqueness of each individual, we create a space where all voices are heard, valued, and respected, fostering an environment of inclusivity and mutual respect.

This celebration of diversity is not just a mere acknowledgment of differences, but a profound recognition of the interconnectedness and interdependence of all beings. It challenges us to step beyond the confines of our own perspectives and embrace the richness that comes from engaging with those who may have different lived experiences. In doing so, we open ourselves up to a world of infinite possibilities, where creativity, innovation, and growth flourish in the fertile soil of diverse perspectives and ideas.

In celebrating diversity and embracing unity in oneness, we affirm our shared humanity and recognize the beauty that arises from the interplay of diverse voices and experiences. It is through this celebration that we pave the way for a more harmonious, compassionate, and interconnected world, where we can truly appreciate the beauty and complexity of the human experience in all its myriad forms.

Living in Oneness: A Path to Peace and Joy

In the tapestry of existence, there is a thread that connects us all. It is the essence of oneness, the realization that we are all part of a greater whole. When we embrace this truth, we open ourselves up to a path of peace and joy that transcends individual desires and boundaries.

Living in oneness is more than just a philosophical concept—it is a way of being in the world. It is a deep recognition of the interconnectedness of all life forms and a commitment to honoring and respecting that interconnection. When we operate from a place of oneness, we see beyond the illusions of separation and division that often plague our world.

In the journey towards oneness, we must first learn to cultivate a sense of unity within ourselves. This means embracing all aspects of our being—our light and shadow, our strengths and weaknesses—with love and acceptance. It requires us to let go of judgment and embrace compassion, both for ourselves and for others.

As we deepen our understanding of oneness, we begin to see the world through a different lens. We recognize the beauty and divinity in all beings, and we treat them with the reverence and kindness they deserve. Our actions become infused with love and compassion, creating a ripple effect of positivity and healing in the world around us.

Living in oneness also means finding balance and harmony within ourselves. It involves honoring the interconnectedness of our mind, body, and spirit, and finding ways to nurture and care for each aspect of our being. Through practices like meditation, yoga, and mindfulness, we can cultivate a sense of inner peace and alignment that radiates outwards.

Ultimately, living in oneness is about co-creating a new reality with the universe. It is about recognizing our power to shape our lives and the world around us through our thoughts, words, and actions. When we operate from a place of oneness, we tap into a wellspring of creativity and inspiration that allows us to manifest our highest potential.

In embracing oneness, we celebrate the diversity and unity that exists within and around us. We honor the unique gifts and talents that each individual brings to the table, while also recognizing the common threads that connect us all. This celebration of diversity in unity allows us to create a more harmonious and inclusive world for all beings.

Living in oneness is a transformative journey that leads to a deep sense of peace and joy. It is a path that invites us to transcend our limitations and embrace the infinite possibilities that lie within us. As we walk this path together, may we find solace in the interconnectedness of all life forms and the beauty of unity in diversity.

In the depths of our being, the concept of oneness stretches beyond the boundaries of time and space, inviting us to dive into the infinite ocean of interconnectedness. As we navigate this profound realization, we come to understand that every thought, action, and emotion we emit ripples out into the vast tapestry of existence, shaping the world around us in ways we may not fully comprehend.

At the core of oneness lies a profound sense of unity that transcends individual identities and egos. It is a recognition that we are all threads in the same cosmic fabric, each weaving our unique story into the grand design of the universe. When we awaken to this truth, a deep sense of peace and harmony washes over us, guiding us towards a more compassionate and inclusive way of being in the world.

In the intricate dance of life, we find ourselves both the dancers and the dance, intertwined in a symphony of energy that flows seamlessly between us and all living beings. This dance of oneness invites us to surrender to the rhythm of the universe, to let go of our need for control and instead embrace the interconnected web of life that cradles us in its loving embrace.

As we journey deeper into the realms of oneness, we begin to see the world with new eyes—eyes that recognize the divinity in every being, the sacredness of every moment, and the beauty that lies in the tapestry of diversity that surrounds us. It is a vision that transcends differences and unites us in a shared experience of love, compassion, and interconnectedness.

Living in oneness is not just a destination to reach, but a continuous journey of self-discovery and growth. It requires us to cultivate a deep sense of inner peace and compassion, to nourish our connection with the higher aspects of our being, and to extend our love and kindness to all beings, regardless of their background or beliefs.

In this grand tapestry of existence, we are but humble weavers, crafting our stories with the threads of oneness that bind us all together. May we embrace this sacred truth, may we dance to the rhythm of unity that pulsates through the cosmos, and may we find solace and joy in the interconnected nature of all life forms.

Living a Life Aligned with Divine Love and Purpose

Living a Life Aligned with Divine Love and Purpose

In this section, we delve into the profound concept of living a life aligned with divine love and purpose. We explore how connecting to the divine source of love allows us to navigate our life's journey with grace and intention. By recognizing and embodying the essence of love within ourselves, we open ourselves up to experiencing a deeper sense of fulfillment and harmony.

Living a life aligned with divine love involves a willingness to let go of fear, judgment, and ego-driven desires. It requires us to cultivate a sense of compassion, forgiveness, and acceptance towards ourselves and others. Through practicing kindness and empathy, we can create a ripple effect of positivity and healing in the world around us.

Furthermore, aligning with our divine purpose means following our inner calling and listening to our intuition. By tuning into our soul's desires and aligning our actions with our higher self, we can create a life that is meaningful and fulfilling. This involves letting go of societal expectations and instead following the path that resonates most deeply with our true essence.

Truly embracing divine love involves understanding that it is a force that transcends human limitations and connects us to something greater than ourselves. It is a force that flows through all living beings and unites us in a web of interconnection. When we recognize this universal love within us and around us, we can tap into a wellspring of compassion and empathy that allows us to see the inherent divinity in all things.

In addition to love, aligning with our divine purpose requires us to delve deep into our innermost being and uncover the unique gifts and talents we possess. Our purpose is not something imposed on us by external forces, but rather a calling that arises from the depths of our soul. By listening to the whispers of our heart and following the path that brings us the most joy and fulfillment, we can align ourselves with our true purpose and make a meaningful contribution to the world.

Living a life aligned with divine love and purpose is a transformative journey that invites us to shed layers of conditioning and ego identification in order to reveal the radiant essence of our true selves. It requires courage, vulnerability, and a deep commitment to self-discovery and self-awareness. But in exchange, we are rewarded with a life that is rich in meaning, connection, and a profound sense of oneness with the universe.

As we continue on this journey of alignment, we may encounter challenges and obstacles that test our resolve and commitment to living in alignment with divine love and purpose. These challenges serve as opportunities for growth and transformation, allowing us to deepen our understanding of ourselves and the world around us.

Through regular practices such as meditation, prayer, or contemplation, we can strengthen our connection to the divine source of love and guidance within us. By quieting the mind and opening our hearts to receive the wisdom and grace that flows through us, we can align ourselves more fully with our true purpose and divine essence.

In essence, living a life aligned with divine love and purpose is a continual process of self-discovery, transformation, and service to others. It is a sacred journey that calls us to embody the highest virtues of compassion, kindness, and authenticity in all that we do. By aligning ourselves with the divine blueprint that animates our existence, we can live a life that is infused with meaning, purpose, and a deep sense of love that transcends all boundaries and limitations.

"What you focus on you create more of, so if the plan is to get rich, you're gonna want to focus on abundance as much as possible. Give as much as you can as often as you can, receive with gratitude and joy, think of money as your pal, raise your frequency and get in the flow, yo."
— Jen Sincero

CHAPTER 8

Get Your Mind Right To Get Your Money Right

Understanding the Power of the Mind in Financial Success

In order to achieve financial success, it is essential to understand the power of the mind and how our thoughts and beliefs influence our financial outcomes. Our minds are incredibly powerful tools that can either work for us or against us in our pursuit of wealth.

The concept of mindset is crucial when it comes to finances. Our beliefs about money, success, and abundance play a significant role in shaping our financial reality. If we hold limiting beliefs or negative attitudes towards money, we may unknowingly be sabotaging our chances of achieving financial success. On the other hand, if we cultivate a positive and empowering mindset, we can attract wealth and abundance into our lives.

It's important to recognize that thoughts have energy and vibration. When we focus our thoughts on lack, scarcity, or fear, we are sending out vibrations that repel wealth and prosperity. Conversely, when we focus on abundance, prosperity, and success, we attract these energies into our lives.

One powerful tool for harnessing the power of the mind in financial success is visualization. By vividly imagining our desired financial outcomes and truly believing in their possibility, we can program our minds to work towards achieving those goals. Visualization can help us stay focused, motivated, and aligned with our financial aspirations.

Additionally, the practice of affirmations can be incredibly beneficial in reprogramming our minds for financial success. By repeating positive, empowering statements about wealth, abundance, and prosperity, we can overwrite any negative beliefs that may be holding us back from achieving our financial goals.

Another key aspect of understanding the power of the mind in financial success is the idea of self-worth. Our self-worth and self-esteem are closely tied to our financial success. If we believe deep down that we are not deserving of wealth or abundance, we may unknowingly be repelling opportunities for financial growth. By cultivating a sense of self-worth and deservingness, we can open ourselves up to receive the abundance that is rightfully ours.

Furthermore, the concept of mindset also includes the importance of goal setting and taking consistent action towards financial success. Setting clear, specific financial goals and breaking them down into actionable steps can help us stay focused and motivated on our path to wealth. By consistently taking small actions towards our financial objectives, we are reinforcing positive beliefs and programming our minds for success.

Moreover, the power of the mind in financial success extends to the realm of gratitude and abundance. Cultivating a mindset of gratitude for the wealth and resources we currently have can attract more abundance into our lives. By appreciating the financial blessings we already possess, we are signaling to the universe that we are ready to receive even more abundance.

In conclusion, understanding and harnessing the power of the mind in financial success is essential for anyone seeking to achieve wealth and abundance. By cultivating a positive mindset, practicing visualization and affirmations, recognizing our self-worth, setting clear goals, taking consistent action, and embracing gratitude, we can tap into the incredible potential of our minds to create a life of financial prosperity and fulfillment.

Breaking Free from Limiting Beliefs About Money

In addition to exploring our beliefs about money, it is important to delve into the root causes of these beliefs and how they may have been formed. Our early experiences with money, such as how it was handled in our households or how it was viewed by our primary caregivers, can have a lasting impact on our financial mindset. For example, if money was often a source of tension or stress in your family, you may have subconsciously absorbed the belief that money equates to conflict or struggle.

Furthermore, societal messages and cultural norms also play a significant role in shaping our beliefs about money. From a young age, we are bombarded with images and stories that link wealth to attributes such as power, success, and happiness. However, these messages can be conflicting, as we are also exposed to narratives that demonize the pursuit of wealth or portray wealthy individuals as corrupt or morally bankrupt.

The impact of media and advertising on our perception of money cannot be overstated. Advertisements often promote a consumerist mentality, encouraging us to equate material possessions with personal worth or happiness. This constant barrage of messages can create a sense of inadequacy or lack, leading us to believe that we need to acquire more to be truly fulfilled.

Moreover, the fear of failure or rejection can also contribute to our limiting beliefs about money. The prospect of taking risks or stepping outside of our comfort zone financially can be daunting, especially if we have been conditioned to believe that success is reserved for a select few or that our worth is tied to our financial status.

To overcome these deeply ingrained beliefs, it is essential to engage in a process of self-reflection and inner exploration. This can involve identifying the specific events or experiences that have shaped your money mindset, acknowledging any fears or insecurities you may have around money, and challenging the validity of your limiting beliefs.

By cultivating a sense of awareness and mindfulness around your beliefs about money, you can begin to shift towards a mindset of abundance and possibility. Embracing a mindset of abundance involves trusting in the abundance of the universe, believing in your own worthiness to receive wealth, and releasing any attachment to scarcity or lack.

Through consistent practice and commitment to transforming your beliefs about money, you can pave the way for a profound shift in your financial reality. By aligning your thoughts, emotions, and actions with a mindset of abundance, you can attract wealth and prosperity into your life and create the financial freedom and security you desire.

Unpacking Childhood Messages About Wealth

As we navigate our journey towards financial success, it is crucial to examine and unpack the childhood messages we received about wealth. Our early experiences and the beliefs instilled in us during our forma-tive years can have a significant impact on how we view money and success as adults.

Many of us grow up hearing phrases like "money doesn't grow on trees," "rich people are greedy," or "you have to work hard to make a living." These messages, whether directly stated or implied, can shape our subconscious understanding of money and abundance.

We may have witnessed our parents or guardians stress about bills, argue about finances, or express anxiety around money. These experiences can imprint on us deeply and create a sense of scarcity or fear when it comes to our own financial well-being. Similarly, if we grew up in an environment where material wealth was idolized or equated with success, we may have developed a distorted view of money and its role in our lives.

Furthermore, societal influences, such as media portrayals of wealth and success, can also contribute to our beliefs about money. From movies to advertising to social media, we are bombarded with images and narratives that can perpetuate harmful stereotypes or unrealistic expectations about wealth.

It is essential to recognize these ingrained beliefs and understand how they may be limiting our potential for financial growth. By delving into our past and reflecting on the attitudes towards money we absorbed in our youth, we can begin to challenge and reframe these beliefs.

Through introspection and self-awareness, we can identify any destructive or restrictive narratives we have internalized about wealth. By acknowledging and confronting these messages, we can start the process of releasing their hold on us and creating new, empowering beliefs around money and prosperity.

Unpacking our childhood messages about wealth is a critical step towards cultivating a healthy money mindset and opening ourselves up to greater financial abundance. By examining and reshaping our early conditioning, we can lay the foundation for a more prosperous and fulfilling relationship with money and success.

Our upbringing shapes not only our beliefs about money but also our overall relationship with abundance and success. The interactions we witnessed between our caregivers and money, as well as the cultural attitudes towards wealth prevalent in our communities, all play a role in influencing our mindset around financial matters.

For some individuals, growing up in an environment where money was a source of tension and stress can lead to a deep-seated fear of scarcity. This fear can manifest in behaviors such as hoarding money, avoiding financial risks, or feeling unworthy of financial prosperity.

On the other hand, individuals who were raised in an environment where money was equated with status and success may struggle with feelings of inadequacy if they do not achieve the same level of financial wealth as their peers or role models. This pressure to measure up to external standards of success can create a sense of constant comparison and dissatisfaction.

Understanding the impact of our childhood messages about wealth allows us to break free from these patterns and create a healthier relationship with money. By acknowledging the influence of our past experiences and actively working to challenge and reframe our beliefs, we can pave the way for a more empowered and abundant financial future.

In essence, by unraveling the tangled web of our upbringing and its impact on our money mindset, we can step into a new paradigm of financial freedom and abundance. The journey towards financial success begins with self-awareness and a willingness to explore and redefine our deeply ingrained beliefs about wealth and prosperity.

Shifting from Scarcity to Abundance Mindset

In exploring the profound metamorphosis from a scarcity mindset to an abundance mindset, it becomes evident that this shift extends far beyond the realm of finances and material wealth. At its core, the transition from scarcity to abundance represents a fundamental shift in consciousness, a reconfiguration of deeply ingrained beliefs and thought patterns that shape one's perception of reality and their place within it.

The scarcity mindset, rooted in the fear of lack and limitations, permeates every aspect of an individual's life, influencing not just their relationship with money but also their approach to relationships, health, creativity, and overall well-being. It manifests as a pervasive sense of inadequacy, driving individuals to constantly seek more in a never-ending quest for security and validation. However, this mindset only serves to perpetuate a cycle of dissatisfaction and discontent, as one is caught in a perpetual state of striving and never truly feeling fulfilled.

On the other hand, the abundance mindset embodies a profound sense of trust in the inherent abundance of the universe and one's own capacity to create and attract prosperity in all its forms. It is a state of being grounded in gratitude and appreciation for the abundance that already exists in one's life, recognizing that true wealth lies not just in material possessions but in the richness of experiences, relationships, and personal growth.

Cultivating an abundance mindset demands a willingness to confront and challenge limiting beliefs that have been deeply entrenched over time. It requires a conscious effort to reframe thoughts and language in ways that align with the principles of abundance, fostering a mindset of possibility, opportunity, and joy. By embracing an abundance mindset, individuals open themselves up to a world of infinite potential, where success and fulfillment are not scarce commodities to be hoarded but abundant gifts to be shared and celebrated.

Moreover, the transition to an abundance mindset is not merely an individual endeavor but also a collective shift that has the power to transform entire communities and societies. When more individuals operate from a place of abundance, the energy of generosity, collaboration, and creativity ripples outwards, inspiring others to do the same. In this way, the ripple effect of abundance can lead to a harmonious and thriving world where all beings can flourish and prosper.

In conclusion, the journey from scarcity to abundance is a profound and transformative odyssey that transcends mere accumulation of wealth and possessions. It is a journey of self-discovery, empowerment, and liberation, where one liberates themselves from the shackles of fear and lack to embrace the boundless possibilities that await in the realm of abundance. By taking the courageous step to shift from scarcity to abundance, individuals pave the way for a life of abundance in all its forms, where joy, love, and fulfillment flow freely and abundantly like a river that never runs dry.

Embracing the Philosophy of Think and Grow Rich

In this expanded exploration of Napoleon Hill's transformative philosophy as elucidated in "Think and Grow Rich," we delve deeper into the intricate tapestry of principles and practices that underpin the journey to success and prosperity. At the core of Hill's teachings lies the potent notion that our thoughts possess the power to shape our external reality. By harnessing the energy of our minds and aligning our thoughts with our deepest desires, we can evoke the forces of the universe to conspire in our favor.

Hill emphasizes the crucial role of clarity in defining our goals with precision and unwavering commitment. A clear and vivid mental image of our aspirations serves as a beacon guiding our actions and decisions towards the realization of our dreams. Furthermore, Hill underscores the necessity of cultivating a burning desire for achievement, a relentless passion that propels us forward through challenges and setbacks with unshakable resolve.

An essential component of Hill's philosophy is the cultivation of a positive mental attitude, a mindset that not only perceives obstacles as opportunities but also emanates a magnetic energy that attracts success and abundance. By maintaining an optimistic outlook and nurturing a belief in our own capabilities, we can provoke a self-fulfilling prophecy that materializes our intentions into tangible outcomes.

Central to Hill's teachings is the concept of the Master Mind, a harmonious alliance of like-minded individuals who collaborate and synergize their strengths towards shared objectives. Through the collective wisdom and support of a well-chosen Master Mind group, individuals can exponentially amplify their creative power and accelerate their progress towards wealth and achievement.

Furthermore, Hill accentuates the significance of persistence as a driving force behind sustained progress and ultimate triumph. In the face of setbacks and disappointments, those who persevere with unyielding determination and unwavering faith in their vision are destined to overcome any adversity and emerge victorious.

In conclusion, "Think and Grow Rich" stands as a timeless testament to the transformative potential of the human mind and spirit. By internalizing and applying the profound principles delineated by Napoleon Hill, individuals can unlock the latent power within themselves, transcend limitations, and forge a path towards enduring success and prosperity.

Manifesting Prosperity with the Law of Attraction

In this section, we delve into the powerful concept of manifesting prosperity through the Law of Attraction. The Law of Attraction posits that our thoughts and beliefs have the ability to shape our reality and draw in corresponding outcomes, including financial abundance. By understanding and harnessing the Law of Attraction, we can unlock the potential to cultivate wealth and success in our lives.

To begin manifesting prosperity through the Law of Attraction, it's crucial to take a deep dive into our subconscious programming and beliefs surrounding money. Often, deeply ingrained beliefs about scarcity, lack, or unworthiness can act as barriers to attracting financial abundance. Through introspection and self-awareness, we can identify these limiting beliefs and work on shifting them towards abundance and prosperity.

Visualization is a potent tool in the practice of manifesting wealth. By creating detailed mental images of our desired financial goals and outcomes, we not only clarify our intentions but also send a powerful energetic message out into the universe. Visualizing ourselves living a life of abundance, success, and financial freedom helps to align our subconscious mind with the frequency of prosperity, making it more likely to manifest in our physical reality.

Affirmations play a key role in reprogramming our subconscious mind for prosperity. By repeating positive and empowering statements about wealth and abundance, we can overwrite limiting beliefs and instill new, empowering money mindsets. Affirmations serve as daily reminders of our inherent worthiness and capacity to attract wealth, reinforcing our commitment to living a financially abundant life.

Gratitude is a transformative practice that amplifies our ability to attract prosperity. By focusing on the blessings and abundance already present in our lives, we raise our vibration and open ourselves up to receiving even more. Cultivating a mindset of gratitude shifts our perspective from a place of scarcity to one of abundance, allowing us to attract greater levels of wealth and success.

Taking inspired action is a crucial component of manifesting prosperity through the Law of Attraction. While visualization, affirmations, and gratitude lay the foundation for attracting wealth, it's essential to follow through with concrete steps towards our financial goals. By aligning our thoughts, beliefs, and actions with the frequency of abundance, we signal to the universe our readiness to receive and allow wealth to flow into our lives effortlessly.

In essence, manifesting prosperity through the Law of Attraction is a holistic process that involves aligning our thoughts, beliefs, emotions, and actions with the frequency of abundance. By embracing a mindset of wealth and success, practicing visualization, affirmations, and gratitude, and taking inspired action towards our financial goals, we can tap into the limitless abundance of the universe and manifest the prosperity we desire. Trust in the process, stay committed to your vision, and allow the magic of the Law of Attraction to unfold in your financial life.

Rethinking Masculinity and Materialism

In a world where traditional gender roles have long dictated societal norms, the intersection of masculinity and materialism is a complex and often overlooked topic. Masculinity, as defined by societal standards, has historically been intertwined with power dynamics and the accumulation of material wealth. From an early age, boys are socialized to equate their value with their ability to assert dominance, achieve financial success, and exhibit physical strength. This pressure to conform to rigid expectations of what it means to be a successful man contributes to a culture of competitiveness and materialistic pursuits.

The connection between masculinity and materialism is further perpetuated by media representations, advertising, and peer influences that emphasize the importance of status symbols, luxury goods, and extravagant lifestyles as indicators of masculine prowess. Men are bombarded with messages that link their self-worth to their financial status and possessions, leading to a constant quest for validation through external means.

This toxic cycle not only reinforces harmful stereotypes about masculinity but also perpetuates a culture of emotional suppression and disconnection. Men who equate their value with material success may neglect their emotional needs, suppress vulnerabilities, and prioritize financial gain over meaningful human connections. This can lead to a sense of emptiness, insecurity, and an inability to authentically express themselves.

In order to break free from the confines of toxic masculinity and materialism, it is crucial for men to engage in introspection, challenge societal norms, and redefine their values beyond material wealth. True masculinity lies in cultivating qualities such as empathy, compassion, integrity, and self-awareness, which are essential for building fulfilling relationships, fostering personal growth, and contributing positively to society.

By embracing a new paradigm of masculinity that prioritizes inner virtues over external validations, men can liberate themselves from the limitations of societal expectations and embark on a journey towards self-discovery and authentic living. It is through this shift in mindset and values that men can reclaim their sense of identity, purpose, and fulfillment, free from the constraints of toxic masculinity and materialistic pressures.

Additionally, the intersection of masculinity and materialism also raises important questions about the impact of consumerism on mental health and well-being. The constant pursuit of material possessions as a means to validate one's worth can lead to a never-ending cycle of dissatisfaction and a lack of fulfillment. Men may find themselves trapped in a cycle of striving for more wealth and status, only to realize that true happiness cannot be found in external possessions.

Moreover, the pressure to conform to societal ideals of masculinity and material success can create a barrier to authentic self-expression and emotional intimacy. Men may feel compelled to suppress their emotions, vulnerabilities, and true selves in order to fit into the narrow definition of what it means to be a successful man. This emotional suppression can have detrimental effects on mental health, leading to feelings of isolation, anxiety, and depression.

To overcome these challenges, men must actively challenge traditional notions of masculinity and materialism, and instead, prioritize self-awareness, emotional intelligence, and vulnerability. By cultivating a deeper connection with their inner selves and embracing authenticity, men can transcend the limitations of societal expectations and forge more meaningful and fulfilling relationships with themselves and others.

In essence, the journey toward redefining masculinity and materialism is a deeply introspective and transformative process that requires men to confront societal norms, question their values, and prioritize inner growth and well-being. By breaking free from the constraints of toxic masculinity and materialistic pressures, men can unlock their true potential, find greater fulfillment, and contribute positively to a more balanced and authentic expression of masculinity in society.

Redefining Success Beyond Money and Possessions

As a celebrated author who has traversed the rugged terrain of success, I have delved into the labyrinthine depths of the human spirit and the essence of achievement. Beyond the sleek façade of glamour and ostentation, I have uncovered the profound essence of triumph, woven from the threads of self-discovery, resilience, and a poignant connection to the collective consciousness that propels us forward on our journey through the tapestry of existence.

In the tumultuous landscape of our contemporary world, the siren call of opulence and power often obscures the profound layers of what it truly means to lead a life of genuine fulfillment. The ceaseless quest for external accolades and tangible markers of success can beguile us with their glittering allure, leading us down a labyrinthine path of illusory gratification and hollow triumphs that leave us yearning for a deeper, more enduring satisfaction.

Through the kaleidoscope of my experiences, I have borne witness to the transformative power of success rooted in authenticity, empathy, and unwavering integrity. It is not in the accumulation of material wealth or the attainment of fleeting accolades that we find true fulfillment, but in the cultivation of meaningful connections, acts of compassion, and a profound sense of purpose that transcends the constraints of mere worldly achievements.

The symphony of success, when played with the harmonious notes of genuine human connection, selfless service, and a steadfast commitment to growth, resonates with a timeless melody that reverberates through the chambers of the heart. It is in the tapestry of our shared experiences, the bonds we forge, and the indelible mark we leave on the fabric of humanity that we discover the true measure of our prosperity and the legacy we are destined to create.

In embracing a holistic perspective of triumph, we unlock the boundless potential that lies dormant within us, casting off the shackles of superficial gratification to embrace a more expansive vision of prosperity that encompasses not only our individual well-being but also the collective flourishing of our global community. As we imbue our endeavors with the essence of authenticity, empathy, and service to others, we illuminate the path for future generations to follow, guiding them towards a brighter, more luminous future filled with the richness of shared experience, compassionate connection, and enduring significance.

Cultivating a Spiritual Connection for Financial Abundance

In this section, we delve even deeper into the intricate relationship between spirituality and financial abundance, uncovering the profound ways in which these dimensions intersect and influence one another on a conscious and subconscious level.

At the core of the spiritual perspective on wealth lies the recognition that true abundance is not solely defined by material possessions or financial success, but by the richness of one's inner world and connection to something greater than oneself. By cultivating a sense of spiritual abundance through practices such as gratitude, meditation, and self-awareness, individuals can tap into an infinite source of wealth that transcends the limitations of money and external circumstances.

The concept of abundance consciousness plays a pivotal role in shaping individuals' beliefs and behaviors around money. When individuals approach wealth from a place of scarcity or fear, they inadvertently block the flow of prosperity into their lives. By shifting towards a mindset of abundance, characterized by trust, openness, and a willingness to receive, individuals can create a receptive vessel for financial blessings to flow into their lives effortlessly.

Moreover, the spiritual pathway to financial abundance involves aligning one's material pursuits with higher values and intentions. By infusing financial goals and decisions with principles such as integrity, compassion, and conscious stewardship, individuals can create a sense of alignment and purpose that enriches not only their bank accounts but also their sense of meaning and fulfillment.

In exploring the societal and cultural dimensions of money and spirituality, we uncover the deeply ingrained narratives and paradigms that shape our collective beliefs around wealth and success. By questioning and transcending societal conditioning, individuals can reclaim their power to redefine wealth in a way that is aligned with their deepest values and aspirations, creating a more conscious and transformative relationship with money.

Ultimately, the integration of spirituality and financial abundance is a journey of self-discovery and transformation, inviting individuals to explore the interconnectedness of all aspects of life and to embrace a holistic approach to prosperity that honors both the material and spiritual dimensions of existence. By embodying the principles of abundance consciousness, integrity, and alignment, individuals can unlock the true potential for wealth and fulfillment that resides within each of us.

Living in Alignment with Wealth and Purpose

In a world where wealth and material possessions often define success, it can be easy to lose sight of our true purpose. Living in alignment with both wealth and purpose requires a deep understanding of oneself and a willingness to prioritize fulfillment over financial gain alone.

To truly live in alignment with wealth and purpose, one must first embark on a profound journey of self-discovery. This journey involves delving deep into one's core values, beliefs, and passions to unearth the essence of their being. It requires introspection and reflection to uncover the unique purpose that lies within each individual.

Identifying one's purpose is not always a straightforward task. It may require exploration, trial and error, and a willingness to embrace uncertainty. But through this process, individuals can uncover the driving force behind their actions and aspirations, providing them with a compass to navigate life's complexities.

Once one has discovered their purpose, the next step is to align their actions with their values. This entails making conscious choices that honor their long-term goals and aspirations, even when faced with challenges or temptations along the way. It requires integrity, perseverance, and a commitment to staying true to oneself, no matter the circumstances.

Living in alignment with wealth and purpose also involves cultivating a mindset of abundance and gratitude. This mindset recognizes the inherent richness of life beyond material possessions – the richness of relationships, experiences, personal growth, and spiritual connection. By focusing on the abundance already present in one's life, individuals can cultivate a sense of fulfillment that transcends monetary wealth.

Furthermore, self-care and self-love play a pivotal role in maintaining a healthy relationship with both wealth and purpose. Taking care of one's physical, emotional, and mental well-being is essential for sustaining the energy and clarity needed to pursue one's goals with passion and resilience. Practices such as mindfulness, meditation, exercise, and nurturing relationships can help individuals nurture a positive and balanced relationship with themselves.

In essence, living in alignment with wealth and purpose is a holistic journey that involves aligning one's values, actions, mindset, and self-care practices to create a life of depth and meaning. By embracing self-discovery, integrity, gratitude, and self-care, individuals can cultivate a sense of purpose that transcends material wealth and leads to a life rich in fulfillment and authenticity.

"*The best way to find yourself is to lose yourself in the service of others.*"
— Mahatma Gandhi

CHAPTER 9

The Joy Of Being In Service

Embracing the Spirit of Service

As a writer, I have always believed in the power of words to inspire, educate, and uplift others. But beyond the pages of my books, I have also discovered the profound impact that acts of service can have on individuals and communities.

Embracing the spirit of service means recognizing the inherent value in giving back to others. It is about understanding that our actions, no matter how small, can make a difference in someone else's life. Whether it's volunteering at a local shelter, mentoring a young person, or lending a helping hand to a neighbor in need, service brings a sense of fulfillment and purpose that goes beyond personal gain.

When we embrace the spirit of service, we open ourselves up to new perspectives and experiences. We learn to see the world through the eyes of others, to empathize with their struggles and celebrate their victories. Service teaches us humility and gratitude, reminding us of the interconnectedness of all beings and the power of compassion.

In a society that often values individual success above all else, embracing the spirit of service is a radical act of kindness and generosity.

It is a way of saying to the world, "I see you, I hear you, and I am here to help." It is a reminder that true fulfillment comes not from what we accumulate for ourselves, but from what we give to others.

The beauty of service lies in its ability to transcend personal differences and bring people together in a shared sense of purpose. When we reach out to those in need, we break down barriers of fear and misunderstanding, fostering a sense of unity and solidarity among all members of society. Through service, we come to realize that we are not alone in our struggles and triumphs, but part of a larger community that thrives on mutual support and kindness.

Service is not just a one-time gesture but a way of life that can transform both the giver and the receiver. It encourages selflessness, empathy, and a deep connection to the needs of others. By stepping outside of ourselves and giving to those who are less fortunate, we cultivate a sense of purpose that goes beyond personal achievement.

As you embark on your own journey of service, remember that the impact of your actions may ripple far beyond what you can imagine. Embrace the spirit of service with an open heart and a willingness to make a difference in whatever way you can. Your efforts, no matter how small, have the power to change lives and create a more compassionate and connected world for us all.

Finding Your Why in Giving Back

In our journey of giving back, it is essential to delve into the depths of our motivations and aspirations, seeking to unearth the profound reasons behind our actions. Discovering your "why" in the realm of service and philanthropy is a journey of self-discovery and introspection, inviting you to explore the very essence of your being and purpose.

As you ponder the driving force behind your desire to make a positive impact on the world, consider the intricate tapestry of your life experiences, values, and beliefs that have woven together to shape your ethos of giving. Is it a poignant personal encounter that stirred a deep sense of compassion within you? Is it a moral imperative engrained in you from a young age, instilling a steadfast commitment to social responsibility? Or is it the unwavering belief that each individual deserves dignity, respect, and opportunity in their pursuit of a fulfilling life?

Your why in giving back transcends mere altruism; it is a profound reflection of your innermost convictions and convictions, a testament to the core of your identity as a bearer of empathy, justice, and transformation. Rooted in the fertile soil of your values, your why serves as a North Star guiding your philanthropic endeavors, lending them purpose, direction, and impact.

By delving deep into the well of your why, you unearth a wellspring of inspiration and resilience that sustains you through the winds of adversity and uncertainty. It is this intrinsic understanding of your purpose in service that empowers you to persevere in the face of challenges, to stand tall against injustice, and to extend a hand of support to those in need with unwavering conviction.

As you navigate the vast seas of social change and community betterment, let your why be the anchor that grounds you, the compass that steers you, and the beacon that illuminates your path towards a more just, compassionate, and equitable world. Embrace your why in giving back, for in its depths lies the transformative power to shape not only the lives of others but also the very essence of who you are and who you aspire to be.

Unleashing Your Unique Gifts for Others

In a world where individuality is celebrated and valued, it is essential to recognize and embrace our unique gifts to make a meaningful impact on others. Each of us possesses a distinct set of talents, skills, and passions that can be harnessed to serve and uplift those around us.

Unleashing your unique gifts for others involves a process of self-discovery and self-acceptance. It requires introspection to identify what makes you stand out and what brings you joy. By recognizing your strengths and acknowledging your limitations, you can cultivate a sense of purpose that drives you to use your gifts for the benefit of others.

Our unique gifts are like pieces of a puzzle, each one fitting together to create a beautiful tapestry of humanity. When we embrace our individuality and share our gifts with others, we contribute to the richness and diversity of the world around us. No gift is too small or insignificant; every act of kindness, every moment of generosity, has the power to inspire and uplift others in ways we may never fully comprehend.

Sharing our unique gifts with others is not just about giving back or making a difference; it is also a form of self-expression and personal growth. When we engage in acts of service or creative expression that align with our talents and passions, we open ourselves up to deeper levels of fulfillment and connection. By using our gifts to connect with others and contribute to the greater good, we tap into a wellspring of joy and purpose that is boundless and transformative.

As we navigate the complexities of life and the challenges that come our way, it is easy to lose sight of the power and beauty of our unique gifts. Yet, it is precisely during these times of struggle and uncertainty that our gifts can shine brightest, offering hope, comfort, and inspiration to those in need. By embracing and sharing our individuality with courage and authenticity, we not only enrich the lives of others but also cultivate a sense of resilience and inner strength that sustains us through the darkest of times.

In a world that often seeks to homogenize and diminish our uniqueness, the act of unleashing our gifts for others is a revolutionary act of defiance and love. It is a testament to the infinite creativity and potential that resides within each of us, waiting to be unleashed and shared with the world. So, let us not hold back or shrink away from our gifts, but instead, let us boldly and unapologetically shine our light for all to see.

Embracing our unique gifts is not just a way to impact others; it is also a profound way to connect with our true selves. By tapping into our individuality and sharing our gifts authentically, we not only enrich the lives of those around us but also deepen our understanding of who we are at our core. Our unique gifts are not just external abilities or talents; they are reflections of our innermost passions, values, and essence. When we share these gifts with the world, we are not only extending a hand of kindness and support to others but also revealing the depths of our own humanity and soul.

In the journey of unleashing our gifts for others, we may encounter challenges and doubts that threaten to dim our light. It is during these moments of uncertainty that we must lean into our uniqueness even more fiercely, embracing our gifts with unwavering confidence and belief in their transformative power. Our gifts have the ability to inspire, heal, and create change in ways that ripple outward and touch lives far beyond our immediate reach. By fully embracing and sharing our unique gifts, we become agents of transformation in a world hungry for authenticity, compassion, and connection.

So, let us not hold back our gifts out of fear or insecurity; let us instead step boldly into our individuality and share our light with the world. For in each of us lies a wellspring of potential and possibility waiting to be unleashed for the betterment of all. The world is waiting for your unique gifts – so go forth and shine brightly, for the impact you make may be far greater than you ever imagined.

The Power of Volunteering

Volunteering is a transformative act that transcends individual boundaries and brings about positive change in society. It is a selfless expression of compassion and empathy that has the potential to reshape communities and inspire individuals to lead lives of purpose and generosity.

When one chooses to volunteer, they are embarking on a journey of connection and service that goes beyond mere altruism. Volunteering is an opportunity to bridge divides, foster understanding, and sow the seeds of empathy in a world often fractured by differences. By engaging with people from diverse backgrounds and lending a helping hand without expectation of reward, volunteers cultivate a sense of unity and belonging that transcends social barriers.

Moreover, the act of volunteering is a powerful catalyst for personal growth and development. Through volunteer work, individuals have the chance to hone their skills, discover hidden talents, and challenge themselves in new and unfamiliar situations. The learning and growth that result from volunteering extend far beyond the immediate impact of the service provided, fostering resilience, adaptability, and a broader perspective on life.

At its core, volunteering is an expression of humanity at its best. It is a testament to the inherent goodness and potential for kindness that exists within each individual. When one volunteers, they are not only offering support and assistance to those in need but also embodying the values of compassion, generosity, and solidarity that are essential for building a just and inclusive society.

The profound effects of volunteering are not limited to the immediate beneficiaries of the service but reverberate throughout the entire community. By inspiring others to get involved, volunteering creates a ripple effect of positive change that spreads far and wide, empowering individuals to come together, make a difference, and create a brighter future for all.

In essence, volunteering is a transformative force that has the power to shape our world for the better. It is a reminder of the inherent interconnectedness of all beings and the boundless potential for love and compassion to effect lasting change. So, let us embrace the profound and far-reaching impact of volunteerism, recognizing it as a powerful tool for building a more just, equitable, and compassionate world for all.

Mentoring: A Gift That Keeps on Giving

Mentoring is a transformative process that transcends the boundaries of age, experience, and expertise. It is a dynamic relationship that thrives on mutual trust, respect, and a shared commitment to growth and development. At its core, mentoring is about investing in others, lifting them up, and guiding them on their journey to success.

The mentor, as an experienced guide, plays a pivotal role in the mentoring relationship. They bring a wealth of knowledge, insights, and wisdom accumulated through their own experiences. By sharing their expertise and offering guidance, mentors empower their mentees to navigate challenges, seize opportunities, and unlock their full potential.

Moreover, mentors serve as role models, embodying the values of integrity, resilience, and continuous learning. Through their actions and words, mentors inspire their mentees to strive for excellence, embrace challenges, and never stop growing. The mentor's impact extends far beyond the realm of professional development, shaping the mentee's character, values, and worldview.

On the other hand, the mentee stands to gain immensely from the mentoring relationship. By receiving personalized guidance, support, and encouragement, the mentee can accelerate their growth, enhance their skills, and broaden their horizons. Mentoring provides a safe space for the mentee to explore their aspirations, confront their fears, and chart a path to success with the mentor's unwavering support.

Furthermore, mentoring is a reciprocal process, benefiting both parties in profound ways. While the mentor imparts knowledge and expertise, they also learn from the fresh perspectives, innovative ideas, and unique experiences of their mentee. This exchange of insights and wisdom creates a dynamic synergy that enriches the mentoring relationship and fosters mutual growth and development.

In essence, mentoring is a gift that keeps on giving, enriching the lives of both the mentor and the mentee. Through the power of mentorship, individuals can forge deep connections, foster personal and professional growth, and contribute to a culture of learning, collaboration, and empowerment. Embracing mentoring is not just about sharing knowledge—it is about creating a legacy of guidance, support, and inspiration that will endure for generations to come.

Making a Difference Through Non-Profit Work

In today's fast-paced and often self-focused world, the act of giving back through non-profit work stands out as a powerful way to make a difference in the lives of others. Non-profit organizations play a crucial role in addressing social issues, providing support to those in need, and promoting positive change within communities.

Volunteering your time and skills to a non-profit organization can have a profound impact on both the recipients of the services and on yourself. By dedicating yourself to a cause greater than yourself, you have the opportunity to contribute to the greater good and help create a more equitable and compassionate society.

Non-profit work allows individuals to get involved in a variety of ways, whether through direct service, fundraising, advocacy, or organizational support. Each role within a non-profit organization plays a vital part in fulfilling the mission of the organization and making a positive impact in the community.

Through non-profit work, you can develop valuable skills, expand your network, and gain a deeper understanding of social issues facing our world today. Whether you are passionate about environmental conservation, social justice, education, health care, or any other cause, there is a non-profit organization out there that aligns with your values and interests.

By getting involved in non-profit work, you have the opportunity to be a changemaker and help create a better world for future generations. Your contributions, no matter how big or small, can make a significant difference in the lives of those who are most vulnerable and in need of support.

Non-profit organizations often serve as a bridge between government entities and grassroots efforts, filling gaps in services and advocating for systemic change. They work tirelessly to address complex social issues such as poverty, homelessness, access to education, healthcare disparities, environmental conservation, mental health support, and more.

The impact of non-profit work extends far beyond the immediate beneficiaries of their services. By addressing root causes of social problems, non-profit organizations strive to create lasting change and empower individuals to improve their own lives. This approach not only benefits individuals in need but also strengthens communities as a whole.

Furthermore, non-profit work fosters a sense of connection and empathy among individuals from diverse backgrounds. It provides a platform for people to come together, share their talents and resources, and work towards a common goal of improving the well-being of others. This sense of community and shared purpose can lead to meaningful relationships and a sense of fulfillment that transcends personal achievements.

In essence, non-profit work is a powerful tool for creating positive social change and fostering a culture of compassion and service. By engaging in non-profit work, you have the opportunity to be a part of something larger than yourself and contribute to the collective effort of building a more just and equitable society for all.

Cultivating Joy Through Service

In the pursuit of happiness, one of the most profound and transformative paths we can embark upon is that of service to others. It is through acts of kindness, generosity, and selflessness that we can truly cultivate a sense of joy that transcends our own personal desires and elevates us to a higher state of being.

Service is not merely a one-sided transaction of giving and receiving; it is a profound exchange of energy and connection that binds us all together in a web of shared humanity. When we extend our hearts and hands to those in need, we not only uplift others but also uplift ourselves in ways that are immeasurable.

The act of service goes beyond simple acts of charity. It encompasses a deep understanding of the interconnectedness of all beings and the recognition that our individual actions have far-reaching consequences in the collective tapestry of life. When we approach service with a mindset of unity and oneness, we tap into a wellspring of compassion and empathy that enables us to see the world through a different lens.

Service also serves as a powerful reminder of our own privilege and the responsibilities that come with it. By acknowledging our own blessings and privileges, we are called to use them for the betterment of others and to contribute to the greater good of society as a whole. This awareness fosters a sense of humility and gratitude that deepens our connection to the world around us.

Through service, we can transcend our own limitations and expand our capacity for love and understanding. It allows us to break down barriers of separation and division, fostering a sense of unity and belonging that is essential for our collective evolution. In serving others, we not only uplift those in need but also uplift ourselves, as we realize that true joy comes from the selfless giving of our time, resources, and energy.

So, as we navigate the complexities of life, let us remember the transformative power of service and the profound impact it can have on our own well-being and the well-being of others. Let us embrace the opportunity to make a difference, no matter how small, and to shine a light in the darkness through acts of kindness, compassion, and love. By embodying the spirit of service, we can create a ripple effect of positive change that reverberates throughout the world, bringing us closer to a more harmonious and compassionate existence.

Overcoming Challenges in Serving Others

One of the profound challenges faced when serving others is that of grappling with the complexities of systemic issues and the structural barriers that perpetuate inequality and injustice. The realization that one's efforts, no matter how well-intentioned, may only be scratching the surface of deep-rooted societal problems can be daunting and disheartening. It can lead to feelings of hopelessness and a sense of futility in the face of seemingly insurmountable obstacles.

To navigate this challenge, it is crucial to maintain a long-term perspective and an understanding of the interconnected nature of social issues. Recognizing that true change requires not just individual acts of service, but also collective action and policy reforms, can help shift the focus from immediate outcomes to broader, systemic change. Engaging in advocacy, community organizing, and policy work can complement individual service efforts and contribute to addressing the root causes of social problems.

Furthermore, acknowledging one's privilege and positionality in relation to those being served is essential in navigating the complexities of service. Being mindful of the power dynamics at play and actively seeking to amplify the voices of marginalized communities can help ensure that service efforts are truly empowering and inclusive. Collaborating with those directly affected by the issues at hand and centering their experiences and perspectives can lead to more effective and sustainable solutions that address the root causes of social problems.

In the face of overwhelming challenges, it is also important to cultivate a sense of resilience and adaptability. Embracing failure as a learning opportunity, rather than a defeat, can foster growth and innovation in one's service work. Seeking feedback, reflecting on experiences, and being open to new ideas and approaches can help navigate obstacles and setbacks with grace and determination.

When faced with the daunting task of serving others in the midst of pervasive social issues, it is crucial to recognize the interconnected web of factors that contribute to the perpetuation of inequality and injustice. Understanding the historical context, systemic structures, and power dynamics that underpin social problems is essential to envisioning effective and sustainable solutions. By digging deeper into the root causes of issues, one can identify points of intervention that have the potential to create lasting change.

Moreover, maintaining humility and a willingness to learn from those directly impacted by social issues is paramount in effective service work. Centering the voices and experiences of marginalized communities can provide invaluable insights and perspectives that may challenge prevailing assumptions and lead to more nuanced and impactful responses. Building authentic partnerships based on trust, respect, and mutual empowerment can foster collaboration and co-creation of solutions that are grounded in shared values and experiences.

In navigating the complexities of service, it is essential to cultivate a sense of empathy, compassion, and solidarity with those facing adversity. Recognizing the humanity and dignity of all individuals, regardless of their circumstances, can inspire a deeper sense of connection and shared responsibility for building a more just and equitable society. By embracing the inherent worth and potential of every person, service efforts can transcend transactional exchanges and foster genuine relationships built on trust, respect, and mutual understanding.

Ultimately, serving others is a multifaceted and transformative journey that demands introspection, collaboration, and a commitment to social justice. By critically examining the systems and structures that perpetuate inequality, amplifying marginalized voices, and fostering empathy and solidarity, one can navigate the challenges of service with grace and resilience, forging a path towards a more equitable and compassionate world.

Building Strong Communities Through Service

Building Strong Communities Through Service

Communities serve as the vital arteries that keep society alive and thriving, connecting individuals in a web of relationships that provide support, belonging, and a sense of purpose. Building strong communities through service is a multifaceted endeavor that goes beyond mere altruism; it is a powerful tool for fostering social cohesion, promoting equity, and driving positive change at both the local and global levels.

At its core, community service is an embodiment of the values of compassion, generosity, and empathy. Whether it is volunteering at a local shelter, organizing a neighborhood clean-up, or participating in a community garden project, individuals who engage in service activities demonstrate a willingness to set aside their own needs and desires to uplift those around them. This spirit of selflessness not only addresses immediate challenges but also cultivates a culture of reciprocity and mutual care that builds bonds of trust and solidarity within the community.

Moreover, service in the community is a catalyst for social change and empowerment. By identifying and addressing systemic issues such as poverty, discrimination, or lack of access to resources, individuals and groups can advocate for policies and practices that promote justice, equality, and sustainability. Through collective action and advocacy, communities can push back against the forces of inequality and injustice, creating a more inclusive and equitable society for all members.

Collaboration and partnership are essential elements of building strong communities through service. When diverse stakeholders come together to tackle common challenges, they can leverage their unique strengths and resources to achieve greater impact than any individual effort. By fostering a culture of shared responsibility and cooperation, communities can build resilience and capacity to address complex problems and navigate uncertain times with confidence and solidarity.

Inclusivity and diversity form the bedrock of strong communities founded on service. It is paramount to create spaces and initiatives that welcome and celebrate people from all walks of life, ensuring that everyone feels valued and respected. By actively promoting equity, cultural diversity, and inclusivity, communities can tap into the full spectrum of human potential, harnessing the creativity and innovation that arise when individuals from different backgrounds come together in pursuit of a common goal.

In conclusion, building strong communities through service is a transformative and enduring process that requires a deep commitment to shared values and collective well-being. By engaging in acts of service, fostering collaboration, advocating for social change, and promoting inclusivity, individuals can contribute to the creation of a more just, resilient, and vibrant community that uplifts and empowers all its members.

Sustaining Your Service Journey

In the continuation of "Sustaining Your Service Journey," it is imperative to delve deeper into the complexities of long-term commitment to serving others. Beyond the initial considerations of personal well-being and boundaries, there is a deeper layer of introspection and self-examination required to truly sustain impact in the realm of service work.

One crucial aspect to explore is the concept of resilience. Resilience is the ability to adapt and bounce back in the face of adversity, which is particularly pertinent in the context of service work. Building resilience involves developing coping mechanisms, cultivating emotional intelligence, and fostering a sense of purpose that transcends challenges and setbacks. By honing these skills, individuals can navigate the inevitable obstacles that arise in service work with grace and perseverance.

Furthermore, it is essential to reflect on the larger societal structures and systemic issues that underpin the need for service work. Recognizing the root causes of social injustices and disparities can inform more effective and sustainable approaches to creating positive change. By advocating for policy reforms, engaging in community organizing, and supporting grassroots movements, individuals can address the systemic issues that perpetuate inequality and bolster their long-term impact in service work.

In addition to personal resilience and systemic analysis, building meaningful relationships with those being served is paramount in sustaining a service journey. Developing authentic connections based on empathy, respect, and trust can create a sense of reciprocity and mutual empowerment in the service relationship. By centering the voices and experiences of those being served, individuals can co-create solutions that address their unique needs and aspirations, fostering sustainable and impactful change.

Ultimately, sustaining a service journey requires a deep commitment to ongoing growth, self-awareness, and social change. By embracing resilience, critically examining systemic issues, and nurturing authentic relationships, individuals can make a lasting impact in the lives of others while staying true to their values and purpose.

> *"Everything Can Be Taken From A Man But One Thing: The Last Of Human Freedoms – To Choose One's Attitude In Any Given Set Of Circumstances, To Choose One's Own Way."*
> – VICTOR FRANKL –

CHAPTER 10

Reasons For Optimism About The Future For Men

In a rapidly changing world where traditional roles and norms are being challenged, there is a growing need to redefine and reimagine what it means to be a man. The outdated notions of masculinity that have long dominated our society are no longer serving us, leading to harmful behaviors and toxic patterns.

It is time to create a new vision for men and masculinity, one that is inclusive, compassionate, and empowering. This new vision acknowledges the diversity of experiences and identities that make up the male experience, recognizing that there is no one-size-fits-all definition of what it means to be a man.

By embracing a more expansive and open-minded view of masculinity, we can begin to break free from the constraints of traditional gender roles and expectations. This new vision encourages men to express themselves authentically, to seek help when needed, and to prioritize emotional intelligence and well-being.

It is a vision that celebrates vulnerability as a strength, promotes healthy relationships built on respect and equality, and challenges toxic behaviors and attitudes that perpetuate harm. By fostering a culture of openness, empathy, and growth, we can create a world where men feel free to be their true selves without fear of judgment or ridicule.

This redefinition of masculinity involves unpacking deep-seated beliefs and biases that have shaped our understanding of gender for generations. It requires introspection and self-awareness to confront and dismantle harmful attitudes and behaviors that have been normalized in society.

Men are not monolithic in their experiences or emotions; they are complex individuals with a wide range of feelings and needs. By recognizing and honoring this complexity, we can create spaces where men can explore and embrace their authentic selves without fear of judgment or rejection.

Part of redefining masculinity also involves examining power dynamics and privilege, understanding how they influence interactions and relationships. Men can use their platform and influence to amplify marginalized voices, advocate for social justice, and challenge oppressive systems that perpetuate inequality.

In essence, reimagining masculinity is about creating a more inclusive and equitable society where all individuals, regardless of gender, can thrive and live authentically. It is a call to action for men to break free from limiting stereotypes and embrace a new paradigm of masculinity that values empathy, compassion, and respect for all.

It is through this introspective journey of self-discovery and growth that men can truly embody a more evolved and holistic understanding of masculinity, one that not only benefits themselves but also contributes positively to the collective well-being of society as a whole.

The Evolving Nature of Men

The evolving nature of men in today's society is a complex and multifaceted phenomenon that reflects a broader shift towards gender equality and inclusivity. As social norms and expectations continue to evolve, the traditional concept of masculinity is being reexamined and redefined to encompass a wider spectrum of behaviors, attitudes, and characteristics.

One of the critical aspects of this evolution is the way in which men are navigating relationships in a changing world. Historically, men were often expected to embody traits associated with dominance, control, and emotional stoicism in their relationships. However, with the gradual dismantling of rigid gender roles, men are now embracing vulnerability, open communication, and emotional intimacy in their connections with others. This shift towards more authentic and egalitarian relationships is fostering greater mutual understanding, respect, and fulfillment for men and their partners alike.

In the realm of work and career, men are also experiencing a transformation in how they define success and fulfillment. The traditional emphasis on power, status, and financial achievement is being complemented by a growing recognition of the importance of work-life balance, mental well-being, and purpose-driven careers. Men are increasingly prioritizing roles that align with their values, passions, and personal growth, leading to a more holistic and fulfilling approach to their professional lives.

Furthermore, the evolving nature of men is evident in the realm of mental health and emotional well-being. For years, men have grappled with societal expectations that dictate they should be strong, resilient, and self-sufficient, often at the expense of their mental health. However, a paradigm shift is underway as men confront the stigma surrounding mental health issues and seek support, therapy, and self-care practices to address their emotional needs. By embracing vulnerability and breaking the silence around mental health challenges, men are not only taking important steps towards their own healing but also contributing to a cultural shift that values emotional intelligence and well-being for all.

In conclusion, the evolving nature of men in today's world signifies a profound reexamination of traditional notions of masculinity and a move towards a more authentic, inclusive, and compassionate expression of manhood. By embracing vulnerability, emotional intelligence, and a holistic approach to success, men are reshaping their identities and relationships in ways that promote personal growth, mutual respect, and societal progress.

Breaking Stigmas: Men Seeking Help and Embracing Therapy

In a society that often places a premium on self-reliance and stoicism, men seeking help and embracing therapy can be a revolutionary act of self-care and vulnerability. Breaking the stigma surrounding men's mental health, this section explores the journey of men who are willing to challenge traditional norms and prioritize their well-being.

For generations, men have been conditioned to suppress their emotions, leading to high rates of untreated mental health issues and a reluctance to seek help. However, shifting cultural attitudes and increased awareness of the importance of mental health have paved the way for men to step forward and confront their inner struggles.

Therapy offers a safe space for men to explore their thoughts and feelings, unpack their past experiences, and develop healthier coping mechanisms. By engaging in therapy, men can gain valuable insights into their behavior patterns, cultivate self-awareness, and find healing from past traumas.

Moreover, seeking help is not a sign of weakness but a courageous choice that demonstrates self-awareness and a commitment to personal growth. Men who embrace therapy not only prioritize their own well-being but also set a positive example for others in their lives, encouraging open conversations about mental health and emotional expression.

As more men recognize the value of therapy and break free from the confines of toxic masculinity, a new narrative of strength and resilience is emerging. By seeking help and embracing therapy, men can embark on a transformative journey of self-discovery, healing, and empowerment, ultimately fostering healthier relationships with themselves and those around them.

The journey of men in therapy also sheds light on the complex intersections of masculinity, vulnerability, and mental health. Traditional notions of masculinity often emphasize traits such as strength, independence, and emotional restraint, creating barriers for men to express their vulnerabilities and seek help when needed.

However, as men engage in therapy and challenge these ingrained beliefs, they pave the way for a more inclusive and compassionate understanding of what it means to be a man. By embracing vulnerability and prioritizing their mental health, men can redefine masculinity on their own terms, dismantling harmful stereotypes and creating space for authentic self-expression and emotional well-being.

In the therapy room, men have the opportunity to unravel the layers of conditioning that have shaped their identities and beliefs about themselves. Through introspection and guided support, they can explore the root causes of their struggles, confront internalized shame and guilt, and cultivate a deeper sense of self-compassion and acceptance.

The impact of men seeking therapy reverberates beyond their individual journeys, influencing societal norms and expectations around men's emotional well-being. By challenging the status quo and advocating for their mental health, men not only transform their own lives but also contribute to a larger movement towards destigmatizing help-seeking behaviors and promoting a culture of open communication and support for all genders.

In essence, the journey of men in therapy is a powerful testament to the resilience and courage it takes to confront inner demons, embrace vulnerability, and prioritize personal growth. Through their willingness to seek help and rewrite their narratives, men are breaking free from the constraints of toxic masculinity and forging a path towards wholeness, authenticity, and emotional liberation.

Men who embark on this journey not only heal themselves but also pave the way for a more compassionate and inclusive society where emotional well-being is valued across all genders. Their willingness to challenge societal expectations and prioritize their mental health is a beacon of hope for future generations, laying the foundation for a more emotionally intelligent and empathetic world.

The Rise of Men's Coaching Industry

In recent years, there has been a significant rise in the men's coaching industry as more men seek guidance and support in various aspects of their lives. Men's coaches offer a unique perspective and tailored guidance to help men navigate challenges, set goals, and grow personally and professionally.

These coaches often focus on areas such as self-improvement, career advancement, relationship dynamics, and emotional intelligence. They provide tools and strategies to help men develop a deeper understanding of themselves and others, improve communication skills, and build resilience.

The rise of the men's coaching industry reflects a growing recognition of the need for men to have a safe space to explore their emotions, vulnerabilities, and aspirations. By working with a coach, men can gain valuable insights, break through limiting beliefs, and unlock their full potential.

Men's coaches play a vital role in supporting men in creating more fulfilling and balanced lives. Through coaching, men can cultivate greater self-awareness, enhance their relationships, and achieve their personal and professional goals. This industry is well-positioned to help men thrive in today's complex world and redefine traditional notions of masculinity.

Furthermore, men's coaches often incorporate mindfulness practices, emotional intelligence training, and goal-setting techniques into their sessions to help men develop a holistic approach to self-improvement. They encourage men to explore their values, beliefs, and priorities, fostering a deeper sense of purpose and fulfillment.

Moreover, men's coaching also addresses the unique challenges and pressures that men face in society, such as societal expectations of masculinity, work-life balance, and mental health stigma. Coaches provide a non-judgmental and empathetic space for men to express their feelings, fears, and aspirations, empowering them to embrace vulnerability and seek growth.

In essence, the men's coaching industry is a valuable resource for men seeking to enhance their personal development, achieve their goals, and lead more authentic and meaningful lives. By tapping into the guidance and support of a men's coach, men can embark on a transformative journey of self-discovery, empowerment, and growth.

Men's coaches play a crucial role in challenging traditional notions of masculinity and encouraging men to embrace a more expansive and holistic view of themselves. This shift towards a more mindful and emotionally intelligent approach to personal development can lead to enhanced well-being, healthier relationships, and greater overall success in various areas of life.

Additionally, men's coaches often explore deeper themes such as identity, purpose, and values with their clients. By delving into these core aspects of a man's being, coaches can help men gain a profound understanding of themselves and align their actions with their authentic selves.

One of the key benefits of men's coaching is the emphasis on self-care and emotional well-being. Many men have been socialized to prioritize productivity and performance over their own mental and emotional health. Men's coaches work to shift this paradigm by helping men cultivate practices that promote resilience, emotional balance, and self-compassion.

Furthermore, men's coaching can also address issues related to communication and conflict resolution, particularly in intimate relationships. By teaching men effective communication skills and conflict management strategies, coaches can help improve the quality of their relationships and foster deeper connections with their partners.

Overall, the men's coaching industry serves as a guiding light for men seeking to evolve, grow, and thrive in all aspects of their lives. Through introspection, guidance, and support, men can embark on a journey of self-discovery, empowerment, and transformation that leads to a more fulfilling and authentic existence.

Men's Groups: Building Supportive Communities

In recent years, there has been a noticeable shift in the way men approach their mental health and well-being. Traditionally, men have been socialized to suppress their emotions, adhere to rigid stereotypes of masculinity, and avoid seeking help for their struggles. However, the rise of men's groups as a support system has challenged these outdated norms and created space for men to redefine what it means to be a man in today's society.

Within these men's groups, individuals find a sense of belonging and community that is often lacking in their everyday lives. The support and camaraderie fostered in these spaces allow men to lower their guard, share their vulnerabilities, and connect on a deeper level with others who understand their experiences. This sense of camaraderie is crucial for men, as it provides a safe and non-judgmental environment where they can be authentic and vulnerable without fear of ridicule or rejection.

Moreover, men's groups serve as a platform for personal growth and self-discovery. Through open and honest dialogue, men can explore their beliefs, confront their insecurities, and reflect on their behaviors. This introspection leads to a greater understanding of oneself and others, fostering empathy, compassion, and emotional intelligence. By engaging in practices such as mindfulness, meditation, and reflective journaling, men can develop greater self-awareness and cultivate a deeper connection to their inner selves.

In addition to personal growth, men's groups also offer a space for men to deconstruct harmful notions of masculinity and societal expectations. By dismantling toxic stereotypes and challenging traditional gender roles, men can embrace a more authentic expression of themselves and cultivate healthy relationships with others. These groups encourage men to redefine strength as vulnerability, to view emotions as a source of power, and to prioritize mental well-being as essential to their overall health.

The impact of these men's groups goes beyond individual growth. By fostering a culture of open communication and vulnerability, men are encouraged to confront their own biases, prejudices, and misconceptions about masculinity. Through dialogue and shared experiences, men can unlearn harmful behaviors, challenge oppressive systems, and actively work towards creating a more inclusive and equitable society. This collective introspection and action are crucial steps in dismantling the patriarchy and promoting gender equality for all individuals.

Ultimately, the rise of men's groups signifies a broader shift towards redefining masculinity in a more holistic and compassionate way. By embracing vulnerability, empathy, and self-awareness, men can cultivate healthier relationships, promote mental well-being, and contribute to a more just and equitable society for all genders. The transformative power of men's groups lies not only in individual healing but in collective action towards dismantling harmful societal norms and fostering a more inclusive and empathetic world for future generations.

Embracing Vulnerability: Redefining Masculinity

In a world where societal expectations often dictate that masculinity is synonymous with strength, independence, and emotional stoicism, the concept of embracing vulnerability as a key component of manhood presents a critical paradigm shift. Men have long been conditioned to suppress their emotions, to bury their vulnerabilities beneath a facade of toughness, in fear of being perceived as weak or inadequate. However, the true strength lies in one's ability to acknowledge, explore, and embrace vulnerability as an integral part of the human experience.

To redefine masculinity to encompass vulnerability is to challenge ingrained norms and redefine what it means to be a man in today's society. It requires a willingness to confront societal norms that equate vulnerability with weakness and recognize that true strength lies in authenticity and emotional honesty. By allowing themselves to be vulnerable, men can embark on a profound journey of self-discovery and personal growth.

Embracing vulnerability empowers men to cultivate deeper connections with themselves and others. It fosters empathy, compassion, and understanding, enhancing their ability to communicate authentically and form meaningful relationships. By dismantling the barriers that inhibit emotional expression, men can foster a greater sense of intimacy and connection in their interactions with loved ones, friends, and colleagues.

Moreover, vulnerability is not a sign of fragility but rather a testament to one's courage and resilience. It takes strength to acknowledge one's vulnerabilities and confront them with honesty and grace. By embracing vulnerability, men can cultivate a profound sense of self-awareness and emotional intelligence, enabling them to navigate life's challenges with greater depth and insight. In essence, redefining masculinity to include vulnerability is a transformative process that liberates men from the confines of traditional gender roles and empowers them to embrace their authentic selves. It is an invitation to transcend societal expectations and cultivate a more compassionate, empathetic, and genuine expression of masculinity. Embracing vulnerability is not a sign of weakness but a celebration of human complexity, a testament to the richness and depth of the masculine experience.

By embracing vulnerability, men can break free from the limitations of toxic masculinity and embrace a more holistic and integrated sense of self. It allows for a more balanced approach to navigating life's challenges, acknowledging that vulnerability is not a sign of weakness but a reflection of our shared humanity. Through vulnerability, men can forge deeper connections with others, fostering a sense of community and belonging that transcends traditional notions of masculinity.

Furthermore, embracing vulnerability can lead to a profound sense of personal growth and transformation. By facing their vulnerabilities head-on, men can tap into a wellspring of inner strength and resilience that enables them to navigate life's uncertainties with grace and courage. It is through vulnerability that profound emotional healing and growth can occur, enabling men to shed the constraints of societal expectations and embrace their true, authentic selves.

In conclusion, embracing vulnerability as a cornerstone of masculinity is a radical act of self-love and acceptance. It is a courageous journey of self-discovery and transformation that empowers men to embrace their full range of emotions and experiences. By redefining masculinity to include vulnerability, men can cultivate a more compassionate, empathetic, and authentic expression of themselves, fostering deeper connections with others and a greater sense of fulfillment and purpose in their lives.

Navigating Relationships with Empathy and Respect

In this section, we further explore the multifaceted nature of empathy and respect within evolving masculinity and the impact they have on interpersonal relationships. As men continue to navigate the complexities of redefining masculinity in a changing world, the importance of cultivating empathy and respect as foundational principles in relationships becomes increasingly evident.

Empathy, a cornerstone of emotional intelligence, involves not only understanding another person's emotions but also experiencing and connecting with those emotions on a deeper level. This ability to empathize allows men to bridge emotional gaps and foster genuine connections with others, leading to increased understanding, compassion, and support within relationships.

Moreover, empathy serves as a catalyst for effective communication and conflict resolution in relationships. By listening attentively to others, acknowledging their perspectives, and responding with empathy, men can create a space where differences are understood, conflicts are addressed constructively, and relationships are strengthened through mutual understanding and shared vulnerability.

Respect, on the other hand, is a fundamental principle that underpins healthy and equitable relationships. Beyond mere politeness or courtesy, respect involves recognizing and valuing the autonomy, boundaries, and inherent dignity of others. By treating others with respect, men demonstrate their commitment to equality, fairness, and mutual regard, fostering a sense of trust and safety within relationships.

In the context of evolving masculinity, challenging traditional gender norms and stereotypes is essential for promoting empathy and respect in relationships. By rejecting toxic masculinity ideologies that prioritize dominance, aggression, and emotional suppression, men can embrace a more authentic and compassionate expression of their masculinity, one that values empathy, vulnerability, and emotional honesty in their interactions with others.

By cultivating empathy and respect in their relationships, men can contribute to a culture of kindness, understanding, and mutual support, where emotional connections are nurtured, differences are celebrated, and individuals feel seen and valued for who they are. Through ongoing self-reflection, growth, and active engagement, men can continue to transform their relationships into spaces of empathy, respect, and connection, where all individuals can thrive and flourish authentically.

From Domination to Collaboration: Challenging Patriarchal Ideals

In a world where patriarchal norms have long dictated societal structures and expectations, challenging these ideals has become a crucial point of discussion in redefining masculinity. The shift from domination to collaboration involves recognizing the harmful effects of traditional power dynamics and striving towards more equitable relationships between individuals of all genders.

Men are encouraged to explore how their actions and beliefs may contribute to perpetuating patriarchal systems, and to actively work towards dismantling them. This may involve acknowledging privilege, actively listening to marginalized voices, and advocating for gender equality in all aspects of life.

By challenging patriarchal ideals and embracing collaboration, men can contribute to creating a more inclusive and equitable society for all. This shift not only benefits individuals by fostering healthier relationships and a greater sense of connection, but also contributes to building a more just and harmonious world for future generations.

Breaking free from the constraints of traditional masculinity is not only liberating for men themselves but also for society as a whole. Men are no longer expected to conform to rigid stereotypes that limit their emotional expression, empathy, and vulnerability. By embracing a more expansive and inclusive view of masculinity, individuals of all genders can cultivate deeper connections and foster a more compassionate and understanding world.

This process of redefining masculinity goes beyond personal growth; it is a revolutionary act that challenges the very foundations of a patriarchal society. By questioning and dismantling harmful gender norms, men can actively participate in creating a more just and equitable world where everyone has the opportunity to thrive and be their authentic selves. This journey towards redefining masculinity is a powerful force for social change and a testament to the transformative potential of embracing collaboration over domination.

Diving deeper into the complexities of this transformation, it is essential to consider the intersectionality of gender with other facets of identity such as race, class, sexuality, and ability. Men from diverse backgrounds may experience masculinity in distinct ways, shaped by the intersections of privilege and marginalization. Understanding and acknowledging these intersecting identities is crucial in fostering a more nuanced and inclusive approach to redefining masculinity.

Moreover, the process of unlearning ingrained patterns of behavior and belief requires ongoing self-reflection, humility, and a willingness to engage in uncomfortable conversations. Men must confront their own biases and resistances to change, while also challenging the broader structures that uphold patriarchal ideals. This journey towards greater awareness and growth demands patience, persistence, and a commitment to justice and equity for all.

As men navigate this transformative path towards redefining masculinity, they may encounter resistance and pushback from those invested in maintaining the status quo. However, standing firm in their commitment to collaboration and equity, men can become powerful agents of change, inspiring others to join them in creating a more inclusive and compassionate world for everyone.

In conclusion, the journey towards redefining masculinity as a shift from domination to collaboration is a profound and multifaceted process that holds the potential to transform individuals, relationships, and societies. By embracing a more inclusive and equitable vision of masculinity, men can dismantle harmful power dynamics, foster deeper connections, and contribute to a more just and harmonious world for all.

Seeking Fulfillment Over Fame: The Quest for Purpose

In today's fast-paced and competitive world, the pursuit of fame and external recognition often takes center stage in our lives. From a young age, many of us are conditioned to believe that success is measured by our achievements, wealth, and status in society. We are encouraged to chase after material possessions and accolades, seeking validation from others as a way to define our worth.

However, as we grow older and gain life experience, many of us come to realize that the quest for fame and external validation is ultimately unfulfilling. The emptiness that accompanies the incessant pursuit of external validation can leave us feeling hollow and disconnected from our true selves. We may find ourselves wondering what the purpose of our life truly is and seeking a deeper sense of fulfillment that goes beyond fleeting moments of fame and recognition.

This shift in perspective often marks the beginning of a journey towards seeking purpose in our lives. We begin to question the values and beliefs that have been ingrained in us and start to explore what truly brings us joy and meaning. Instead of chasing after external markers of success, we start to listen to our inner voice and follow our hearts to pursue what truly matters to us.

Seeking fulfillment over fame means prioritizing our well-being, relationships, personal growth, and contribution to the world. It involves aligning our actions and choices with our values and beliefs, and living a life that is authentic and meaningful to us. It requires us to cultivate self-awareness, empathy, and compassion towards ourselves and others, and to approach life with a sense of curiosity and openness.

The quest for purpose is not always easy or straightforward. It requires us to confront our fears, insecurities, and limiting beliefs, and to step outside of our comfort zones in order to discover what truly lights us up. It involves taking risks, making bold choices, and following our intuition even when the path ahead is unclear.

Ultimately, the journey towards seeking fulfillment over fame is a deeply personal and individual one. It is about honoring our unique gifts and talents and using them to make a positive impact in the world. It is about finding joy and satisfaction in the present moment, rather than constantly chasing after some distant goal or external validation.

As we embark on this quest for purpose, we may face challenges and setbacks along the way. There may be moments of doubt, confusion, and uncertainty, but it is through these struggles that we grow and evolve into the best versions of ourselves. The journey towards seeking fulfillment over fame is not always easy, but it is a journey worth taking, as it leads us towards a life that is rich in meaning, purpose, and contentment.

This inner journey towards self-discovery and fulfillment requires a willingness to embrace vulnerability and authenticity. It involves peeling back the layers of societal expectations and uncovering our true desires and passions. It is a process of redefining success on our own terms and learning to celebrate our unique strengths and qualities.

In this quest for meaning, we may find ourselves drawn to experiences that challenge us, inspire us, and bring us closer to our true selves. Whether it's through creative expression, deep relationships, acts of service, or personal growth, each step we take towards aligning our lives with our values brings us closer to a sense of fulfillment that transcends the fleeting highs of external validation.

As we navigate the complexities of modern life, with its pressures and distractions, the pursuit of purpose becomes a grounding force that anchors us in times of uncertainty and change. It reminds us of what truly matters and guides us towards a life that is rich in meaning and significance. And as we continue on this journey, we discover that the true measure of our success lies not in the fleeting praise of others, but in the deep sense of peace and fulfillment that comes from living an authentic and purposeful life.

Mental Health and Wellness for Men

Mental health and wellness for men are crucial components of their overall well-being, encompassing the complex interplay of biological, psychological, and social factors. Men's mental health needs have long been overlooked or misunderstood, contributing to a pervasive culture of silence and stigma surrounding their emotional well-being.

The traditional expectations of masculinity have often constrained men's ability to express vulnerability and seek help for mental health concerns. The dominant societal narratives around masculinity emphasize characteristics such as strength, stoicism, and self-reliance, creating barriers for men to openly acknowledge their emotional struggles and access the support they need.

Moreover, the intersection of gender norms, race, sexuality, and socioeconomic status can further compound the challenges that men face in addressing their mental health. Men from marginalized communities, such as men of color or LGBTQ+ individuals, may experience additional stressors and barriers to care, leading to disparities in mental health outcomes.

The impact of untreated mental health issues among men is profound and far-reaching. Research has shown that men are less likely than women to seek help for psychological distress, leading to higher rates of undiagnosed and untreated mental health conditions. This reluctance to address mental health concerns can result in serious consequences, including an increased risk of substance abuse, relationship difficulties, and suicide.

However, there is a growing recognition of the need to challenge traditional notions of masculinity and promote a more inclusive and compassionate understanding of men's mental health. Initiatives aimed at breaking down stigma, such as public awareness campaigns and community-based programs, are helping to encourage men to prioritize their well-being and seek support when needed.

In recent years, mental health professionals have also developed tailored interventions and resources specifically designed to support men's mental health needs. Culturally sensitive therapy approaches, support groups, and online mental health services are increasingly available to provide men with the tools and support they need to navigate their emotional challenges and build resilience.

Physical health practices play a fundamental role in men's mental well-being as well. Regular exercise, proper nutrition, and adequate sleep not only contribute to physical health but also have a profound impact on mood regulation and stress management. Engaging in activities that promote relaxation, such as hobbies, mindfulness practices, and spending time in nature, can also nurture men's mental well-being.

Furthermore, fostering connections and cultivating supportive relationships are essential for men's mental health. Building strong social networks, seeking out mentorship or peer support, and engaging in meaningful conversations with trusted individuals can provide men with a sense of belonging, validation, and emotional support during challenging times.

In conclusion, promoting mental health and wellness for men requires a multifaceted approach that addresses the unique experiences and needs of men across diverse backgrounds and identities. By challenging stigma, expanding access to resources, and fostering a culture of emotional openness and support, we can empower men to prioritize their mental health, cultivate resilience, and lead fulfilling lives.

The Bright Future Ahead: A New Era of Masculinity

In a world where traditional notions of masculinity are being challenged and redefined, there lies a bright future ahead for men. The old stereotypes and expectations that once confined men to narrow roles are giving way to a new era of masculinity that celebrates diversity, emotional intelligence, and authenticity.

As society continues to evolve, so too must our understanding of what it means to be a man. Men are no longer defined solely by their ability to conform to outdated standards of strength and stoicism. Instead, they are encouraged to embrace their vulnerabilities, express their emotions, and cultivate meaningful relationships based on respect and empathy.

The new era of masculinity is characterized by a profound shift towards collaboration and partnership, rather than dominance and control. Men are learning to value qualities such as communication, cooperation, and compassion, recognizing that true strength lies in openness and vulnerability.

Empowered by this shift, men are increasingly seeking fulfillment and purpose in their lives, rather than simply chasing external markers of success. They are prioritizing their mental health and overall well-being, recognizing that self-care is not a sign of weakness, but a necessary aspect of living a balanced and fulfilling life.

Men of all backgrounds are coming together to support one another in this journey of self-discovery and growth. They are creating spaces for open dialogue and vulnerability, breaking down the walls of isolation and stoicism that have long hindered true connection and intimacy.

Within this new era of masculinity, men are redefining what it means to be strong and resilient. They are embracing their emotions, acknowledging their failures and insecurities, and learning to navigate the complexities of modern life with grace and humility.

As men continue to forge a path towards this new era of masculinity, they are paving the way for a more inclusive and equitable society for all. By embracing their authentic selves, challenging harmful norms, and supporting one another in their growth and transformation, men are reshaping the future of masculinity for the better.

The bright future ahead is one where men are free to be their true selves, unburdened by limiting expectations and instead empowered to live authentically and with purpose. It is a future where masculinity is defined by its capacity for compassion, connection, and personal growth—a future that is full of promise and possibility for men of all backgrounds and experiences.

In this new era of masculinity, men are not only embracing their own growth and self-acceptance but are also actively working to dismantle toxic masculinity in society. By challenging harmful behaviors and attitudes, advocating for gender equality, and promoting healthy relationships built on mutual respect and understanding, men are contributing to a more just and compassionate world for all. The journey towards this new masculinity is not without its challenges, as societal norms and expectations are deeply ingrained and can be difficult to overcome. However, through collective effort, support, and a shared commitment to positive change, men are making significant strides towards a future where authenticity, empathy, and vulnerability are celebrated as pillars of true strength. This new era of masculinity is not just a personal transformation for men—it is a societal shift towards greater equality, understanding, and interconnectedness among all individuals.

~~~~~~~~

I began this book by saying the greatest challenge facing our world today is to redefine manhood and masculinity, I also mentioned that this can only be accomplished one man at a time. I hope this book has provided you with some insights to support you in changing your beliefs and attitudes about what it means to be a man. My hope is that you will apply some of the lessons from this book into your own life and in doing so, your life will become more rewarding and fulfilling. If you found this book to be helpful, my request is that you share it with others. The more men we can engage in this dialog, the sooner we can shift the paradigm of masculinity.

Most importantly, be optimistic about the future. Know that humanity always finds a way to evolve and grow, and shifting the paradigm of masculinity is no different. Humanity is waking up, and it is our responsibility as men to wake up to who we truly are and to come together to make the world a better place.

We got this!

Coach Michael Taylor

About Coach Michael Taylor

Michael Taylor is a shining example of resilience and determination, having overcome immense personal challenges to become a renowned life coach, motivational speaker, and bestselling author. His unwavering commitment to empowering others has inspired countless individuals to pursue their dreams and live extraordinary lives.

A former high school dropout, Michael faced seemingly insurmountable obstacles, including divorce, bankruptcy, foreclosure, depression, and even homelessness. Yet, through sheer grit and an unshakable belief in himself, he emerged from these trials as a beacon of hope and inspiration.

With 14 published books under his belt, Michael's words have touched the lives of readers worldwide, guiding them towards personal growth, self-discovery, and the realization of their full potential. As a certified life coach, he has dedicated his life to helping men and women break free from self-imposed limitations and embrace the extraordinary within themselves.

Michael's journey has been a testament to the power of perseverance and the indomitable human spirit. As the president and CEO of Creation Publishing Group, he continues to champion the pursuit of dreams and the creation of a life filled with purpose and fulfillment.

Happily married to his soulmate, Bedra, for over two decades, Michael finds solace and joy in the simple pleasures of life. When he's not empowering others through his writing and coaching, you'll find him indulging in the soulful melodies of 70s and 80s music or immersing himself in the latest cinematic masterpieces.

With an infectious optimism and an unwavering passion for the impossible, Michael Taylor stands as a testament to the boundless potential that lies within each of us. He firmly believes that there has never been a better time to be alive on this planet, and his mission is to inspire others to embrace this belief and live their lives to the fullest.

www.coachmichaeltaylor.com
Email: mtaylor@coachmichaeltaylor.com
Phone: 713-565-0083